Architectural Guide
London

Architectural Guide
London

Twentieth-Century
Housing Projects

Tjerk Ruimschotel

DOM
publishers

Housing projects either side of the 20th century: Peabody Close, built in 1887, and behind it, Peabody Avenue, completed in 2011

The *Deutsche Nationalbibliothek* lists this
publication in the *Deutsche National-
bibliografie*; detailed bibliographic data
are available at http://dnb.d-nb.de.

ISBN 978-3-86922-525-8

© 2021 by DOM publishers, Berlin
www.dom-publishers.com

Copy-editing
Amy Visram

Design
Lupe Bezzina

Maps
Katrin Soschinski

QR codes
Christoph Gößmann

Printing
Tiger Printing (Hong Kong) Co., Ltd.
www.tigerprinting.hk

About the Author

Tjerk Ruimschotel

Tjerk Ruimschotel (born 1949) is a Dutch urban designer, lecturer, and publicist. He trained at Delft University in the late 1960s and early 1970s, and until a few years ago worked for private firms and local councils. Latterly he was chief urban designer of the city of Groningen in the north of the Netherlands. Alongside this, he taught and lectured, carried out research on former Dutch colonial architecture and urbanism in Indonesia, and regularly wrote for professional magazines. He is the co-author of *Atlas of Change: Rearranging the Netherlands* (2001). From 2009 to 2015 he was chair of the Dutch Association of Urban Designers and Planners (BNSP).

Since he is not based in London, Tjerk Ruimschotel has no first-hand experience of living there, though he does frequently visit his daughter, her British husband and their two Anglo-Dutch sons. He never worked professionally as an architect or town planner in London or the United Kingdom and does not claim to know the building industry and policy-making around housing first-hand. As an

Source: Marianne Harbers

urban designer, however, he has always had an interest in British architectural design and especially housing. From his student days onwards, he has regularly visited newly built projects such as the Alton Estates and the construction sites of Barbican and Thamesmead in the 1960s and 1970s. He continues to do this up to the present day, when a new generation of British architects are realising the importance of (social) housing for the living fabric of the city. One of his long-held beliefs is that an outsider's perspective can (at times) be a favourable point of view.

Contents

My home is my castle: a British house par excellence
designed by Ernest Trobridge (see project 022)

Introduction
An Outsider's Guide to 20th-century Housing in London

London has always been a residential metropolis, and when looking at its homes over the twentieth century we can distinguish several fascinating, experimental periods. After the squares of the Georgian period and Victorian terraced housing, the twentieth century began with some significant housing projects inspired by the Arts and Crafts and Garden City movements. During the interwar years, modernist architecture was introduced in London, alongside some art deco complexes. After the Second World War, the extensive construction programme – mostly realised through highrise buildings – saw its countermovement in the low-rise high-density projects of the 1960s and 1970s. After a dip in both quantity and quality during the last decades of the century, the first two decades of the twenty-first century saw a new wave of interest in social housing and residential architecture in general.

This guide focuses on residential architecture during this span of time in London: it begins with the late-nineteenth-century precursors to what is often referred to as council housing and ends with the RIBA National Award-winning Dujardin Mews, completed in 2017. This long stretch of more than 100 years of course encompasses a wide range of styles: Neo-Georgian, Postmodern, Blairite, and New London Vernacular, to name but a few in addition to those already mentioned. However, the structure of this book is based less on architectural style and more on the changing nature of housing problems and the ways in which solutions to these were sought over time. It picks up on experimental approaches and the developments – both built and historical – that they made possible.

Housing in the British capital has always been constructed by either the private or the public sector. The aim of erecting private housing developments has, naturally, always been predominantly speculative. Yet at times such architecture has had a wider impact on housing in general. This guide features both private and public developments: it aims to cover 'domestic architecture for the rich, poor, and those in between'.[1] However, its main subject matter is public housing.

Social Housing

Social housing, more than any other category of architecture, frequently incorporates two poles: to paraphrase the architect Albert Sigrist, it is at the same time capitalistic and socialist, bourgeois and proletarian, autocratic and democratic, private and social. It is no longer individualistic, and even when produced by individual architects, it becomes part of one large body of knowledge and experience. The architecture of dwellings oscillates between 'housing the poor' and providing homes for everyone: it has to be a space within which the occupant may do exactly as they please – 'An Englishman's home is his castle' – and also form part of the collective environment – the city, neighbourhood, street, block and terrace.

In the past, public housing in Britain was often known as 'council housing' because of the role that county and borough councils played in its construction. However, since Registered Social Landlords (RSLs) – a category that includes housing associations of different types – now play a very significant role in building and managing housing, both council and RSL homes are known as 'social housing' – the term used in this guide.

London's Administrative Structure

Historically, developments in housing have been driven by the interrelation between private initiatives and rules and legislation, between laissez-faire policies and government intervention, between fiscal austerity and investment. And London itself has its own very specific history: though always determined by growth, its story is one of concentration versus decentralisation, of intensification versus outward growth, and of the displacement of populations and functions. More than in any other city, the relationship between the administration, its boroughs, and the government of the United Kingdom has been a very particular one (and one reinforced by the peculiarities of the two-party political system). The specifics of this fast-growing metropolis within its surrounding rural area have long shaped its housing. A brief summary of the structure of the local government is therefore a helpful backdrop for understanding the changes that occurred in residential architecture over the course of the twentieth century.

The first elected local authority responsible for housing in the British capital was London County Council (LCC). It was established under the 1888 Local Government Act and was in charge of infrastructure, transport, and housing reform. The LCC's jurisdiction was over what is now known as Inner London. In 1900 a new set of 28 metropolitan boroughs were created, and they adopted some of the powers of the LCC. As the city expanded rapidly over subsequent decades – in particular during the mid-twentieth century – the council could not cope with the extensive demands it faced. When the official London area was expanded significantly in 1965 (Greater London) and the list of boroughs revised, the LCC was abolished and replaced by the Greater London Council (GLC). The GLC itself was dissolved in 1985, and its planning powers were given to central government and committees in the individual boroughs. In 2000, the Greater London Authority (GLA) was established by a referendum: a twofold authority consisting of the London Assembly and a Mayor of London, the first directly elected mayor in the United Kingdom. Today the GLA oversees strategic planning in the Greater London area.

Social Housing in London: Chronology

London's housing stock, constructed as it has been over many centuries, is a subject too vast to deal with without dissecting it into comprehensible parts and periods. Each chapter of this guide therefore deals with a distinct period in the history of housing, either by concentrating on several different moments or by marking out a single event in time.

The period before the First World War was the last architectural period named after the reigning British monarch. Neither Victorian nor Edwardian architecture was defined by a particular style; they both present an eclectic blend of revived historical and foreign styles, all created mostly as a reaction to simple Georgian and symmetrical Palladian architecture. From the mid-nineteenth century to the start of the twentieth century, middle-class housing displayed a mock Tudor (also called Tudorbethan or Tudor Revival) architectural language. A sense of collective, or to be precise, top-down, responsibility for London's housing began to emerge at the beginning of this period. Then, in the last quarter of the century, a number of acts of parliament were passed to improve mass housing. This led to the first British town-planning act: the 1909 Housing and Town-Planning Act, a law that, following the principles of Ebenezer Howard's concept of a garden city, limited the number of dwellings builders could erect on a site with the aim of reducing overcrowding.

The First World War highlighted the inadequacies of Britain's housing. The poor physical condition of the drafted soldiers was blamed on the inadequate conditions in which large sections of society lived. During the conflict, it became apparent that only government-driven and planned housing could produce the required number of homes in the right locations. After the war, there was a need for housing for the soldiers returning from the battlefields – the homes 'fit for heroes' promised by Prime Minister

David Lloyd George in 1918. By building these houses, the government also hoped to avoid uprisings among these young, army-trained men.

Various governmental reports and actions to tackle the acute housing shortage led to extensive suburbanisation. Simple yet improved housing was built in low-density, self-contained communities to garden-city layouts. The 1919 Housing Act – also known as the Addison Act, after its author, the health minister Christopher Addison – gave local authorities the resources they needed to provide public housing.

In contrast to the First World War, which was fought on the continent, the Second World War led to many casualties at home and material damage to London itself. During the war, several papers, such as the *Beveridge Report* (1942) and the *Dudley Report* (1944), anticipated the post-war need for more state-controlled production, in particular in housing. The County of London (1943) and Greater London (1944) plans provided the spatial framework for this new development.

Post-war reconstruction not only had to catch up with a housing-stock deficit; it also had to deal with the expected population growth and increase in prosperity. The yearly construction of council houses reached its peak in 1953, with 220,000 homes erected that year. In its influential 1961 report *Homes for Today and Tomorrow*, the Parker Morris Committee recommended that the quality of social housing should match the rise in living standards. The minimum-space requirements specified for council houses by the committee were influential during the 1960s but less so during the following decade. In the ensuing period, building standards for these dwellings declined somewhat: projects were often situated on the fringes of cities and were high-rise – factors that led to various social problems.

In 1980, Margaret Thatcher's government passed the Local Government, Planning and Land Act, which established urban-development corporations. The most dramatic watershed in the history of housing was the introduction, that same year, of the Right to Buy through the Housing Act of 1980. Through this, Thatcher's government sought to further deregulate the housing market, reduce the cost of housing, and create a country full of homeowners. The difficult economic conditions of the 1990s meant little was built in the latter years of the twentieth century, and the majority of it was far from innovative.

At the start of the twenty-first century, a London-wide government was once again established: the Greater London Authority (GLA). Its London Plan enabled the building boom of the 2000s and guided its construction of offices and the buildings for the Olympic Games in 2012. The housing market was diverse during this period: demolition and renovation went hand in hand, house prices continued to rise, and luxury homes were erected on a large scale. It thus became almost impossible for many sections of the population to buy or rent a house in London. Boroughs and architects experimented with a New London Vernacular. Some people even spoke of an urban renaissance.

In 2017, Dujardin Mews, a social housing project in the borough of Enfield, received a RIBA National Award. This was a signifier that architects had again taken up the task of providing excellent, truly affordable homes. That same year, however, a housing tragedy of unimaginable dimensions occurred: fire broke out in Grenfell Tower, a 24-storey block of flats in west London. This, the worst residential blaze in Britain since the Second World War, left 72 dead, damaged public trust in building regulations, and raised tough questions on not just the safety of this building, but also around the social-housing policies of local and national government – questions that have still not been answered.

Notes:

1   Following the motto of the architectural page of the Victorian Web, an online archive of 'networked' information. See www.victorianweb.org/art/architecture/homes/.

About this Guide

Originally, the aim of this book was to include London's exemplary housing projects: the biggest, best, and most distinctive projects, along with the most innovative and experimental ones, irrespective of their success or failure. As time went on, though, the objective became to gather a representative cross-section of projects that not only provided a good home for their inhabitants but also made a significant contribution to the spatial quality of the surrounding environment. Accordingly, the search was for examples of housing where the architect has turned the idea of a collective housing project into a central element of the design by introducing features that the mere repetition of dwellings does not produce automatically. Often, these projects are well-known in the field of architecture, but not always. Sometimes they have received distinctions and awards within the profession, while at the same time becoming infamous in public opinion and the press. In addition, some projects have an iconic status outside the field of architecture and play an essential role in literature, films, songs, or urban legends.

The main reason for this publication was that it did not exist already. In general, there is not a great deal of organised information on iconic and experimental housing projects, let alone appreciation for innovative, unorthodox projects in the field of housing construction. This guide is not an academic study; it merely tries to make a start with putting together details of relevant projects so readers can position them in space and time. To this end, the guide provides accurate details on the exact location of the project (something that funnily enough is often missing in other guides) and how to travel there by public transport or car – hence the QR code. As far as possible, information is given on the number and type of dwellings, size of site, client and architect in charge, and wherever possible, within a wider context.

Although the hundred or so projects documented here are widely seen to be the most interesting, it was surprising to find how little factual information about these projects is available and how often sources contradict each other. Data had to be obtained from all possible sources. As the content of this publication could not be based on archive study, it had to be marshalled from a wide variety of publications and the internet, which was unashamedly plundered for data and descriptions. Over the four years during which this guide was compiled, all of the projects described in it were visited (along with many more).

The final selection of projects resulted from a juxtaposition of them with those in other architectural guides and in publications on housing and London architecture. When compiling this research, it became clear that mass housing has not been the main focus of architects or historians in London – or for that matter the UK – for some time. Books have recently been published on estates such as the Barbican and Thamesmead and buildings like the Isokon, but most architectural publications still centre around individual architects. Quite a few London architects (deceased or alive and still working) have a monograph dedicated to them – from Wells Coates to Walter Segal – but such titles on significant architects such as Kate Macintosh, Rosemary Stjernstedt, and Ernest Trobridge are still outstanding.

The primary sources were of course the buildings and estates themselves. Next were the listing descriptions at the website of Historic England and the conservation area assessments by the London boroughs. Wikipedia was frequently consulted as a starting point for further exploration. Equally useful was the rather British phenomenon of public information sharing via internet sites and blogs covering a wide range of rare, unusual, or particular data on architecture and housing in London and the UK.

Pre-war

From 1850 to 1914

The most relevant of those online sources are mentioned in the bibliography, and some of the books that have grown out of these blogs are also included in the bibliography. The number of publications dealing with different aspects of housing in Britain or London is growing.

Nevertheless, there is still a clear need for a handy guide that can be used to locate and visit (or at least the former) the housing projects included here – whether it is because they are widely talked about, heavily criticised, justly glorified, or wrongly forgotten.

Source: Tjerk Ruimschotel

Some exemplary social housing is not listed and so runs the risk of being demolished: Central Hill (Lambeth Architects' Department/Rosemary Stjernstedt, 1970–1974)

Parnell House
Streatham Street/
Dyott Street, Camden
Henry Roberts
1849
⊖ Tottenham Court Road

One typology that formed the foundations of twentieth-century social housing in London was the multi-storey apartment block built for the working class in the nineteenth century. It was initially constructed only by charitable societies and then by public authorities from the 1890s onwards. The British architect Henry Roberts (1803–1976) designed several early socially-responsible housing schemes in London. These no longer exist. Examples include the Sailors' Home in Well Street, Whitechapel (1835), the Model Dwellings in Pentonville (1844), and a Model Lodging House near Drury Lane (1846). The latter was erected for the Society for Improving the Condition of the Labouring Classes (SICLC), of which Roberts was a founder member. His Model Houses for Families on Streatham Street, later called Parnell House, is the oldest surviving instance of an apartment building that provides accommodation for the 'deserving poor in regular employment' in London. This U-shape block of dwellings for 48 families was erected around a courtyard in Streatham Street. It has five storeys and a basement with workshops. Access is via one entrance on Streatham Street and open galleries in the courtyard. The galleries are supported by brick piers extending up the height of two floors. They lead into flats comprising, for the most part, two bedrooms, plus a living room, kitchen, and scullery. The introduction of water-closets in each dwelling was exceptional for the time; bath and laundry facilities were still communal. Parnell House was restored in 1956 by Frederick Gibberd & Partners and is now managed by the Peabody housing association who took over the SICLC and all of its remaining London properties in 1965. It was Grade II* listed in 1974.

Source: Bob Bronshoff (all pictures)

Prince Albert's Model Dwellings
Kennington Park Road, Lambeth
Henry Roberts
1852
⊖ Oval

002 E

The original building that housed Prince Albert's Model Dwellings was designed by Henry Roberts and erected in Hyde Park by the Society for Improving the Conditions of the Labouring Classes for the 1851 Great Exhibition. When the building was rejected as an exhibit, Prince Albert (1819–1861), who had interests in both improving the welfare of the poor and the arts, saw to it that the building could be constructed near the exhibition grounds. Roberts designed it to house four families, with each of the two storeys containing two flats. He stated that his design was aimed at 'the class of mechanical and manufacturing operatives who usually reside in towns or in their immediate vicinity'. Each flat had a living room, a kitchen/scullery, three bedrooms, and a toilet. Bathrooms were not usually provided in houses built in England at the time. There were three bedrooms so that children of different sexes would not have to share rooms. Where Roberts' Parnell House had gallery access at the back, the Model Dwellings building introduces a collective entrance connecting the individual flats to the street. Hollow bricks were used for the building, and were stated to be sound and damp resistant, non-porous, and inexpensive to make. The internal surface of the walls was smooth, so plastering was seen as unnecessary. The design provided impetus for further work on model homes, and Roberts and the society produced publications on the subject, such as *The Dwellings of the Labouring Classes* (1850). After the Great Exhibition ended, the building was taken down and rebuilt in its present location near Kennington Park in 1852. It was Grade II* listed in 1961. Since 2003 it has served as the head offices of the charity Trees for Cities.

Source: Philipp Meuser (all pictures)

Peabody Square
Greenman Street, Lambeth
Henry Darbishire
1851

⊖ Oval

Peabody Square on Greenman Street in Islington is the oldest surviving estate belonging to the Peabody charitable housing trust. It was among the first of its kind to focus on the issue of dwellings for the poor while employing a systematic design. The layout of the estate in Islington was new: rather than the more traditional rows of houses along a street, it consists of four freestanding Italianate-style blocks arranged around a central courtyard, a controlled-access space that can serve as a safe play area for children. The Greenman Street Estate proved to be model for the housing of the 'deserving poor' – both for later Peabody estates and social housing in general. Its urban morphology was one of turning away from the clutter of the neighbourhood within a semi-private enclave. Contemporary images portray Peabody Square as a shining island of order in the dark, chaotic mass of the industrial city. Although several philanthropic institutions existed at the time and some had even started to build dwellings, none were to become as successful and influential as the Peabody Trust. Its founder, George Peabody,

was born in 1795 into a large poor family in Massachusetts, USA. He left school early to support his widowed mother and earned his living importing and exporting goods. He made his fortune in merchant banking. Peabody's first trip to Britain was on business in 1827, and a decade later he moved to London, where he stayed until his death in 1869. When it was suggested to him that he could do something to alleviate the extreme poverty in his new hometown by supporting low-rent housing, he set up the Peabody Donation Fund in 1862. It later became the Peabody Trust, and is today known as Peabody. Despite the philanthropic foundations of the trust, the capital it invested had to produce new built projects. Its estates therefore only catered for 'respectable' labourers: those with regular incomes. The first Peabody project was constructed in 1863 on Commercial Street in the Spitalfields area. For it, Henry Darbishire (1825–1899) designed two long housing blocks, situated over shops, on a small and awkward site. Some typical Peabody features could already be seen, including the grouping of the service areas vertically, the limited number of staircases, and the corridor system; however, the central courtyard was absent. The builder was William Cubitt & Co., the firm who erected most of the trust's subsequent estates. The

earliest surviving classic Peabody estate in London is the one on Greenman Street. It was there that the rectangular courtyard was introduced as the organising principle for access and social cohesion. Built in 1865, the scheme originally consisted of four long blocks in a sober style: A, B, C, and D. All are five storeys high. The four standard floors would house two three-room, seven two-room, and one one-room apartment, arranged on both sides of an internal corridor. This, in theory, allowed a household to stay in the same estate as the family needs changed. The apartments were not self-contained; the residents had to share kitchens and lavatories in the narrow ends, which could easily be inspected regularly for cleanliness. The shared toilets and sinks survived up until 1911, when private facilities were introduced. Communal laundries were on the fifth floor with unglazed openings for drying the washing. Next along Greenman Street was Peabody House, the three-storey house for the estate manager, and Peabody Yard, which contained 12 workshops. Residents and visitors enter the estate through a gate at an open corner of the square. In 1885 the project was expanded, with five further blocks – E, F, G, H, and I – erected south of Peabody Square and accessible via the square's open corners. These blocks, bordering Dibden Street, have their address at Greenman Street; there is also a gate that gives access to the estate from Dibden Street. In 1994 Blocks A to D were awarded Grade II listed status. Blocks E to I are not listed at the moment, but they lie within the curtilage of the estate and contribute positively to the overall composition.

Source: Tjerk Ruimschotel (all pictures)

Peabody Estate

Blackfriars Road (opposite no. 150), Southwark
Henry Darbishire
1871

004 C

Southwark

The Peabody Estate on Blackfriars Road is significant in the history of social housing as it was the first such development in south London. Land was more affordable there than it was in the north of the city. The Peabody Trust's sixth estate was more extensive and spacious than the earlier ones. But, as always, it was separated off from the urban network; the only entrance for pedestrians and cars is via a vast classical archway between blocks on Blackfriars Road. The scheme is formed by two courtyards, each comprised of eight roughly identical blocks. They all have a rectangular plan and are four-storeys tall, a modest height in comparison to earlier Peabody developments. Some blocks are joined together to make double blocks. Most are detached, which gives the estate an airy atmosphere. The two courtyards are joined at a 45-degree angle at the corner of the first courtyard. Slightly later, a five-storey block of similar design and plan was built to fill the central space between the two blocks on the southwestern side of one of the courtyards. Two further five-storey blocks were also added to the north, on Blackfriars Road. The number of dwellings on the estate then reached 384. The laundries were housed in separate buildings, rather than in the attics. Initially, there was also a shared bathroom in the basement of nearly every block. Staircases were used as main accessways to flats, as opposed to the corridors employed in earlier estates. The façades of the blocks facing Blackfriars Road are less sober than those of the other blocks: they feature gables and more intricately patterned brickwork. Henry Darbishire designed his standard blocks more as a collection of rooms than as a group of dwellings. At a RIBA meeting in 1875, he stated, 'each storey contains 10 living- and bedrooms so that each block of five storeys contains 50 of these rooms. They are placed together for the purpose of composing dwellings of various sizes, without rendering any structural alteration'.

Peabody Estate: Entrance on Blackfriars Road

Holly Village

Swains Lane, Camden
Henry Darbishire
1865
⊖ Archway

005 B

Holly Lodge was commissioned around fifty years after England's first garden village was built by John Nash in Blaise Hamlet near Bristol (1811). The latter had a wide-ranging influence, which reached the wealthy nineteenth-century philanthropist Angela Georgina Burdett-Coutts (1814–1906). She requested the construction of a dozen rather small yet still highly elaborate houses on a site at a corner of the grounds of Holly Lodge, the country villa of her grandfather Thomas Coutts. Holly Village was designed by Burdett-Coutts's favourite architect, Henry Darbishire, before he became the principal architect for the Peabody Trust. Darbishire's previous work for Burdett-Coutts included an ambitious private development consisting of four blocks around a central open space: Columbia Square, model dwellings for the working class built between 1859 and 1862, and demolished in the 1950s. In recognition of Burdett-Coutts's socially-conscious work, Queen Victoria made her a baroness in 1871. She was also a friend of Charles Dickens, who helped plan Holly Village. The group of twelve Victorian Gothic dwellings consists of four detached

Holly Village: View through the grand entrance gate

houses, six semi-detached cottages, and two gateway cottages flanking a central gabled archway. This entrance archway, which bears the inscription 'Holly Village erected by AGB Coutts AD 1865', leads to the private communal garden, around which the other dwellings are grouped in an orthogonal layout. Costly materials were employed, including Portland stone and teak. Intricate carvings adorn the buildings, while Burdett-Coutts is depicted holding her dog in a statue situated to the left of the entrance. A model venture for 'private rent to those on considerable incomes', Holly Village was, contrary to popular belief, never occupied by estate workers or retired clerks from the bank Coutts & Co. It is one of the oldest gated communities and was purchased by its tenants in 1921. Its architectural importance was recognised as early as 1954, when it was Grade II listed.

1

Bedford Park

The Avenue/Bedford Road,
Ealing and Hounslow
Richard Norman Shaw et al.
1875–1914

006 D

🚇 Turnham Green

Bedford Park was planned as a village-like community situated at a commutable distance from the City of London. It had all of the required public buildings – a church, a public house, shops and schools – and became an inspiration for the Garden Suburb movement of the 1900s. The idea for the community came from Jonathan Carr (1845–1915), a resourceful cloth merchant. Carr was the son-in-law of the engineer Hamilton Fulton, who lived in Bedford House and owned almost 10 hectares of the surrounding land. Realising the numerous possibilities for this area near the new Turnham Green Underground Station, Carr purchased land from Bedford House and two neighbouring homes in 1875. His goal was to give the middle classes appealing dwellings and surroundings, and he therefore incorporated the established trees in the grounds of Bedford House into his plan. Carr, though, was a slightly dubious property developer, and by 1886 he had to stop work on the development. Before that, however, he was successful in publicising the artistic reputation of Bedford Park by employing high-profile designers. He initially commissioned Edward William Godwin (1833–1889), an architect, interior designer, and leading figure of the Aesthetic Movement. But the published designs for the houses attracted severe criticism for being too small and awkward in plan, and only a few were built. In 1877 Carr therefore requested another leading architect of the time to design the suburb: Richard Norman Shaw (1831–1912). Shaw's first drawings for Bedford Park contained streetscapes accommodating more than just houses: wooden boundary fences and other exterior features that prefigure what was actually built. They were an immediate success, establishing the pattern for the architecture in the suburb – and not only for those houses constructed by Shaw. Since Carr had bought the designs,

he was free to use these as a reference for further buildings. By 1880, Shaw had grown tired of Carr and resigned. He was succeeded by his pupils Edward John May (1953–1941) and Maurice Bingham Adams (1849–1933), both of whom also lived at Bedford Park while expanding it by building houses in the manner of Shaw. The other residents were a mixture of high-wage earners and the less well-off. Among them were the French impressionist painter Camille Pissarro (1830–1903) and the family of the poet W. B. Yeats (1865–1939). The poet John Betjeman (1906–1984), the first patron of the Bedford Park Society (an amenity society

founded in 1963), called it 'the most significant suburb built in the last century, probably the most significant in the Western world.' Betjeman's description from 1960 echoed that of the German architect Hermann Muthesius (1861–1927), who in 1904 had written in *Das Englische Haus*, 'There was at the time virtually no development that could compare in artistic charm with Bedford Park ... and herein lays the immense importance of Bedford Park in the history of the English house.' The architectural quality of the estate deteriorated in the period after the Second World War. In 1967 the amenity society organised an exhibition to highlight the history of Bedford Park and the dangers it faced. Among the visitors was an inspector from the Ministry of Housing, who recommended the listing of 356 buildings from the original suburb. Ealing and Hounslow, the two boroughs in which the estate fell, declared their parts of the suburb conservation areas in 1969 and 1970. In 2002 the Bedford Park Society became the first British amenity society to create a database of all its listed buildings and provide every house with a customised logbook. This document details the house's history and instructs the owner on how to approach making alterations or repairs to her or his home.

Redcross and Whitecross Cottages

Redcross Way and 1-6 Ayres Street, Southwark

Elijah Hoole

1887–1890

🔴 Borough

007 C

The Whitecross Cottages (1890) are six two-storey houses situated along Ayres Street. Together with the six two-storey Redcross Cottages (1887), located behind them on Redcross Way, they form a group of buildings that display the influence of the Arts and Crafts Movement and the ideals of Octavia Hill (1838–1912), a social reformer and pioneer of working-class housing. The architect of both sets of cottages was Elijah Hoole (1837–1912), a friend of Hill's who worked with her for 40 years. Hoole also designed dwellings for industrial workers, for which he received medals at international exhibitions. Hill had a strong commitment to alleviating poverty and had her own approach to providing and running social housing. Believing in self-reliance, she became one of the first social-housing managers. Central to her system was the weekly visit to collect rent, a task performed only by female voluntary workers. For Hill, it was essential that she and her assistants knew their tenants personally and could act when the house was overcrowded or when children were not attending school. She was opposed to the governmental provision of housing, viewing it as bureaucratic and impersonal. Hill saw suitable housing and open spaces as being vital for people's health. These two factors were combined in the model ensemble between Ayres and Redcross streets, which includes community buildings (George Bell House and Bishop's Hall) and Redcross Gardens. The latter was open to the urban network of streets, and provided much-needed green space in the crowded city. It was designed by Emmeline Sieveking and Fanny Wilkinson and included an ornamental pond, a bandstand, and a play area. Its official opening ceremony was held in 1888. The project for the ensemble was funded by some prominent women of the time: the politician and trade-union organiser Dorothy Jewson and the wealthy sponsor Lady Jane Dundas. Through fostering well-maintained attractive houses around a village green with a community hall, Octavia Hill may have foreshadowed the main features of turn-of-the-century town planning. Today the cottages are still managed by Octavia Housing, an organisation that emerged from the Horace Street Trust, the housing association founded by Hill.

Source: Tjerk Ruimschotel (all pictures)

1

The Webb Estate

Main entrance on Foxley Lane/
Furze Lane, Croydon
William Webb
1888–1925
🚊 Purley

The Webb Estate is a garden suburb that stretches over 105 hectares in Purley, south London. In 1888, when William Webb (1862–1930), a surveyor and horticulturist, began planning the residential estate, Purley was a village and the surrounding area farmland. Webb created the estate according to his 'Garden First' approach (he later outlined these ideas in *Garden First in Land Development*, published in 1919). For him, the garden was not only more important than the dwelling, but it also had to be landscaped and well-established before the houses could be erected. He therefore set up a nursery to grow trees, hedging, and plants, and began shaping the infrastructure of the estate. The construction of houses began in 1901, when the plants and trees had matured. Developing the estate along these lines took time, and finally finished in 1925. Almost every road on the estate follows a curving path. Some of their names are taken from the planting schemes. Since there were shops in Purley, the only one in the estate was the Lord Roberts, a temperance inn containing the village store and post office, built at the corner of the Upper Woodcote Village Green near the southernmost entrance to the estate. There are also two schools. The four entrances are not connected, which prevents thoroughfare

traffic. Practically all of the 220 houses are large and situated within extensive grounds, except for the semis along Furze Lane. For the garden to maintain its priority over the houses, Webb formulated a number of specific ground rules. These include: 'No house erected on the land shall be used for any purpose other than that of a private residence. No house shall be advertised as or designed for or occupied as flats nor shall any trade, business, profession, school or manufacture be carried out on the said piece of land. Nor shall anything be done that shall become a nuisance or annoyance to the adjoining owners. No building shall be erected within 60 feet of the road or 10 feet of the side boundaries. No part of the land shall be used as a public road or as a means of access to another property. No boundary or party fences or walls shall be erected on the land other than wire fences and live hedges and the purchaser shall do all that be necessary to maintain such parts of the live hedges as are on his ground. The display of contractors advertising boards is not allowed. No clothes, except children's garments, shall be hung out to dry unless hidden by a hedge or other suitable enclosure.' These rules have contributed significantly to the current character of the estate and the Borough of Croydon incorporated some of the key points into its 2007 Conservation Areas Appraisal and Management Plan as guidelines for new development. None of the buildings are listed; however, the estate remains an important early example of a form of town planning that recognised landscape as a primary component for housing.

Brentham Garden Suburb

Bounded by Meadvale Road,
Neville Road, Fowler's Walk,
Winscombe Cresent, Woodfield
Cresent, Pitshanger Lane, Ealing
*Parker & Unwin, Frederic Cavendish
Pearson, George Lister Sutcliffe et al.*
1901–1915
⊖ Hanger Lane

Brentham Garden Suburb is an estate of 650 houses in Ealing, a borough which at the end of the nineteenth century was predominantly rural. It was established by Ealing Tenants Ltd, a cooperative tenants' society which was the first to supply good-quality housing for workers in London. In 1901 the society commissioned more than 100 houses with an Edwardian terrace design. The building work ran until 1906, constituting the first construction phase of the estate. A large proportion of it was carried out by General Builders Ltd, a co-partnership firm owned by Henry Vivian (1868–1930), a trade unionist politician and the chairman of Ealing Tenants Ltd. This phase centred around Woodfield Road, Woodfield Avenue, Brunner Road, and Woodfield Crescent. The first three roads lie at right angles to Pitshanger Lane, and with Pitshanger Lane and the latter, generating a grid pattern softened by the slight bend in Woodfield Crescent. The second phase of Brentham's planning was quite different. It began in 1907 when Raymond Unwin (1863–1940) and Barry Parker (1867–1947) were engaged as

architects for the suburb. The pair had previously worked on Letchworth, the world's first garden city, established in 1903 based on the ideas of Ebenezer Howard (1850–1928). In Brentham, their plans transformed what was a small housing estate into a distinctive garden suburb, and the area was to become a testing ground for their subsequent masterpiece, Hampstead Garden Suburb (010). This second phase exhibits some design principles from the garden-city movement, with softly curving roads following the landscape between Pitshanger Lane and Meadvale Road. To make the streets more varied, Parker & Unwin grouped the houses into varying blocks of four and six units, and kept existing features of the landscape. Their plan included many open spaces for recreation and limited the number of houses. The cottage-style properties all have gardens, and behind some groups of houses there are allotments. Beyond the pioneering urban layout, Parker & Unwin designed only a few houses in this early

Source: Tjerk Ruimschotel (all pictures)

garden suburb (1–7 Winscombe Crescent, 2 Brentham Way). The majority of the houses built from 1907 to 1911 were designed by the young architect Frederic Cavendish Pearson (1882–1963). He was responsible for 135 houses in Brentham (Brunner, Ludlow, Meadvale, Neville and Brunswick roads, Ruskin Gardens, Winscombe Crescent, Pitshanger Lane, one end of Brentham Way). These clearly display the influence of the Arts and Crafts Movement in their detailing. Particularly worthy of note are the butterfly-shaped blocks on the bend of Brunswick Road and two blocks in Ludlow Road with diamond-shaped living rooms. In 1910 George Lister Sutcliffe (1864–1915) took over as the suburb architect, marking the beginning of the third phase of its construction That same year he realised the Brentham Insitute and two years later Holyoake House, a group of small flats around a small green at the end of Holyoake Walk. For the most part, though, he created single-family homes (for instance in Brentham Way, Fowlers Walk, Holyoake Walk, North View,

and Denison Road). The style of his work was more sober than Pearson's. He worked for the development until his death in 1915. Further houses were added in the 1920s (Cecil George Butler), 1930s, (Frank Winter, Alwyn Gorbing, Henry Ward) and 1950s (W. Pack, G. Salter and Sons). Sport and leisure were important features of Brentham. From the very start, the residents had enjoyed well-organised social events, which led to a strong communal spirit, something supporters of cooperative enterprises particularly valued. In 1904 there were already cricket and tennis clubs and a bowling green, and in 1907 recreation grounds were created near the River Brent. The Brentham Institute was officially opened in May 1911 to provide sports facilities and to cater for social events such as lectures and concerts. The institute is the only listed building in Brentham and today houses the Fred Perry Café, named after the tennis champion who lived and played in the suburb. In 1969 the suburb was designated a conservation area.

Hampstead Garden Suburb
Central Square, Barnet
Parker & Unwin
1907–1914
🚇 Golders Green

Architecturally speaking, one of London's best-known housing developments is undoubtedly Hampstead Garden Suburb. It was conceived by the social reformer Henrietta Barnett (1851–1936), who, with her husband Samuel (1844–1913), was involved in trying to improve housing conditions in the East End. Barnett set up the Hampstead Garden Suburb Trust in 1905. The organisation purchased about 100 hectares of land for the scheme. Barnett's original motive for the development was to prevent the conventional practice of filling up the fields around the newly built Golders Green Underground Station with uniform rows of terraced homes. She wanted to provide a variety of salubrious and picturesque dwellings for people from different classes, with the rent brought in by the high-end mansions subsidising the construction of low-rent cottages. She stipulated that it be planned 'not piecemeal but as a whole' and that the grouping of the dwellings enhance variety and irregularity. She appointed Raymond Unwin and his partner Barry Parker to plan the suburb. The two architects had previously drawn the master plan for Letchworth Garden City and worked on Brentham Garden Suburb in Ealing (009), and applied similar ideas in Hampstead: putting in curved roads, retaining landscape features, and providing houses with diverse aesthetics. However, contrary to the usual ideals of the Garden City, 'the Suburb' as it was known to locals, was too small to be self-contained. To achieve some sort of completeness, Barnett and Unwin wanted a civic centre at the top of the hill: Central Square was to be the focal point of the suburb. Its design underwent numerous revisions. Unwin's first sketch for the suburb in February 1905 included communal buildings such as a church, library, and shops, in and around a central village green. Barnett annotated the plan considerably, and the final plan of 1911 for Central Square ended up being rather formal. Two churches face each other on one of the axes of the square, with a further education college centrally placed on the

northern side. Unwin's layout was influenced by medieval towns in the German state of Bavaria, as he later stated in his book *Town Planning in Practice* (1909). He created a street structure that worked with the existing landscape and built houses in cul-de-sacs. However, the by-laws established after the 1875 Housing Act made these innovative urban forms impossible, and it took an act of parliament to allow him to deviate from the

prescribed grid-iron street layout. The Hampstead Garden Suburb Trust therefore sponsored a private bill, which became law as the Hampstead Garden Suburb Act 1906. Building work started in 1907. Unwin's final plan of 1911 (for the first phase of the suburb) was a clever collage of several solutions for diverse spatial (and economic) problems. He designed houses on small strips on both sides of the 30-hectare Hampstead Heath Extension. This green space, planned to block the urbanisation from Golders Green, terminates abruptly at the Great Wall, which forms a clear border with the rectangular layout of the high-end residential quarter surrounding Central Square. Further northwest, the arrangement becomes more loose and picturesque. When the development along Meadway reaches Finchley Road, more than a kilometre north of Golders Green Underground Station, the entrance to the suburb is created by two Bavarian-inspired blocks with shops and apartments. In the 1930s the suburb expanded to the north. By the end of the decade, it covered 400 hectares, with more than 10 per cent of it parkland. This extension is considered to be of less architectural value than the earlier developments. In 1968 the suburb was designated as a conservation area. Today, it houses approximately 12,500 people in just over 5,000 households. First and foremost it is a middle- and upper-class area, and as such has moved away from its original objectives.

Boundary Street Estate 011 C

Arnold Circus and surroundings,
Tower Hamlets
LCC Architects' Department/
Owen Fleming et al.
1894–1900
🚇 Shoreditch High Street
🚇 Old Street

The Boundary Street Estate marked a key step forward in the history of social housing. It was the first large housing estate designed by the Architects' Department of the London County Council (LCC), which was established by an 1888 act of parliament. Within the department, at the time led by Thomas Blashill (1831–1905), the Housing of the Working Classes Branch, formed in 1893, undertook the work. Most of the practitioners there had been trained at London's Architectural Association School of Architecture. Owen Fleming (1867–1955) was in charge of the project at the age of just 26, with Thomas Charlton (1868–1935) and Robert Robinson (1866–1939) serving as chief assistants. In the middle of the nineteenth century, the area bordered by Virginia Road and Mount, Boundary, and Old Nichol streets was an infamous slum spanning more than 6 hectares. The conditions were later vividly described by Arthur Morrison in *A Child of the Jago* (1896), a novel in which he changed the slum's name to 'Jago'. When the Housing of the Working Classes Act of 1890 gave the local government the power to demolish slum housing, the LCC adopted the Bethnal Green Road Improvement Scheme, which covered the clearance of the Old Nichol Street area. Around 5,700 people lived in the slum and had to be rehoused in the new Boundary Street estate. In 1893 the Architects' Department revised an earlier design with an orthogonal layout to provide more residences: over 1,050 dwellings were created. On the plan seven tree-lined streets radiate from a central plaza: Boundary Gardens. This raised public park is contained inside a circular road, Arnold Circus. It was created using the earth excavated for the foundations of the Boundary Estate housing blocks and served as a focal point for the new community. Buildings lined the radial streets. Housing and shops were provided in 20 individually designed blocks in different sizes and shapes. All displayed an Arts and Crafts style. Several architects working at the Housing of the Working Classes Branch were employed for the different blocks. Reginald Minton Taylor (1867–n.d.) was responsible for most of the northern section around Arnold Circus, while Charles Canning Winmill (1865–1945) designed most of the buildings in the southern part. Mostly five-storeys high, the freestanding buildings follow the course of the streets but are constructed in such a way that as much light and air as possible penetrates the area. All living rooms were designed to receive sunlight at some point during the

day. A central laundry was installed; this was deemed more cost-effective than putting facilities in each block. To foster local businesses, workshops were provided for craftspeople and vendors. Calvert Street, the existing road from Shoreditch High Street, was lengthened and widened to serve as the main entrance to the estate and then renamed Calvert Avenue to reinforce its grandeur. Rochelle School and Virginia School pre-dated the development. Although not all the buildings were finished and occupied, the Boundary Street Estate had a prestigious opening ceremony in March 1900, conducted by the Prince of Wales, who a year later would become Edward VII (1841–1910).

It also attracted wide-ranging interest at the time, and its influence spread to housing schemes on the continent. Nevertheless, its success was somewhat limited: it proved costly and in the end only rehoused 4,600 people – not as many as it displaced. This was often the case with slum clearances. Because few of the former slum-dwellers could afford the rents, the LCC later began to examine the possibility of providing low-rise, low-density developments in the suburbs, an idea that was linked to subsidised transport. The London Borough of Tower Hamlets designated the estate as a conservation area in 1985. The 20 blocks are currently Grade II listed.

Source: Bob Bronshoff

011 C

Boundary Street Estate: View of Calvert Avenue
from the raised garden at Arnold Circus

Millbank Estate

Erasmus Street, Westminster
*LCC Architects' Department/
Reginald Minton Taylor*
1897–1902

⊖ Pimlico

The Millbank Estate, designed by Reginald Minton Taylor (1867–n.d.) and others, was the second big project carried out by the London County Council (LCC) Architects' Department. Taylor was responsible for the layout of the estate and most of the social-housing blocks. The estate was built on the octagonal site of the former Millbank Penitentiary, in operation from 1816 to 1890. The Tate Gallery (now the Tate Britain) was also erected on this expansive site. Part of the redevelopment of the area was earmarked for public housing by a Royal Commission in 1885. This proved to be an opportunity to rehouse tenants displaced by slum clearances and the scheme to build Kingsway. The project expanded on LCC's commitment to producing high-quality working-class housing by employing Arts and Crafts principles and the knowledge gained from the Boundary Street Estate (011). Tenants there did not have to share toilet and scullery facilities, but unlike at Boundary Street, there was no communal laundry room. Planned for 4,430 people, the 15 five-storey mansion blocks with spacious courtyards were all individually modelled. The layout of the estate is symmetrical, and the design of the corresponding blocks on either side of the axis of symmetry is identical. The orthogonality of the design is softened by two diagonal streets leading to Millbank Gardens, a long rectangular public garden behind the Tate. Because of this proximity to the gallery, the red-brick blocks are named after British artists, including Turner, Gainsborough, Reynolds, and Ruskin. Millbank Primary School was constructed over the prison graveyard at the same time as the estate. The only reminder of the Millbank Penitentiary (apart from the name) is its old moat in the courtyard of Wilkie House, which was used as the estate's communal drying area. This became a community garden in 2013. The Millbank Estate now comprises 561 individual flats, half of which are occupied by council tenants and half by leaseholders.

Totterdown Fields
Between Church Lane and
Upper Tooting Road,
Wandsworth
*LCC Architects' Department/
Ernest Stone Collins*
1901–1911
⊖ Tooting Bec

013 D

In 1900 a new Housing Act enabled local councils to construct housing outside
their own jurisdiction. This act enabled
London County Council (LCC) to look further afield for land to fulfil an old wish:
to provide cottages with gardens for
working-class households. The cheaper
land on the outskirts of London could accommodate these 'cottage estates' better than the inner-city areas. Though others such as White Hart Lane (now known
as Tower Gardens [014]) and Norbury
were built 'out county', Totterdown
Fields was erected just on the edge of

LCC's administrative area. The plans for
Totterdown, drafted by Ernest Stone
Collins (1874–1942), included 1,244 cottages. These were divided into four different classes: from five-room homes (first
class) to homes divided into two three-
room flats, one on the ground floor and
the other on the first floor (fourth class).
When the estate was completed in 1911,
it contained 1,261 cottages on an area of
15 hectares. The streets are arranged in
a grid pattern, with three shorter roads
crossing four longer roads aligned on a
northwest-southeast axis. The longer
streets curve so as to permit pleasant vis-
tas along the rows of houses. Each row
is one large building yet is marked out
as individual by its detailing. This dis-
plays the architects' desire to present
the groups of houses as singular yet still
part of a consistent whole through common materials and patterns. When the
estate was planned, it was foreseen as

Source: Tjerk Ruimschotel (all pictures)

the largest such development in Tooting. However, the drawings omitted schools, churches, and parks (such facilities were being planned nearby) and only featured four shops at the centre of the estate. Totterdown therefore had more in common with a garden suburb than Ebenezer Howard's self-sustaining garden city.

Tower Gardens

Between Tower Gardens Road
and Risley Avenue, Haringey
LCC Architects' Department/
William Edward Riley et al.
1904–1914

014 A

🚇 White Hart Lane ⬡ Wood Green

In April 1901, London County Council (LCC) purchased 90 hectares of 'out-county' land between White Hart and Lordship lanes in Tottenham. The ability to buy land outside the LLC's administrative area to house London's rapidly growing population had been introduced by the 1900 Housing Act. On the land, the LCC built accommodation for 33,000 people – about the same number Ebenezer Howard stipulated as the ideal population of a garden city. In total, 963 two-storey cottages were erected from 1904 to 1915, when work stopped due to the lack of workers and materials caused by the First World War. Construction started again in 1920 and continued until the late 1930s. The estate was initially called White Hart Lane, but the pre-war part later became known by the name of its park, Tower Gardens. Its lead architect was William Edward Riley (1852–1937), the LCC's chief architect at the time. Assisted by others in the Architects' Department, he designed a cottage estate that

followed the same lines as other such developments (Totterdown Fields, for instance [013]): it displayed the influence of the Arts and Crafts and Garden City movements in its green spaces and humble yet detailed and diverse houses. The houses, built in red and yellow London stock brick and lime mortar, featured various different types of sash window and prominent chimney stacks. The layout comprised 12 short streets between the straight Risley Avenue and the slightly curved Tower Gardens Road. In the eastern part, some cross-streets make way for a sort of village green, surrounded by raised walkways and gardens. This public space, now known as the Tower Gardens Recreation Ground, as well as the low density of the buildings, was made possible through a donation from the banker and Liberal politician Samuel Montagu (1832–1911). The 10,000 pounds sterling was given on condition that it be used to relocate disadvantaged residents of Whitechapel (Montagu was MP for Whitechapel from 1885 to 1900), an area in the borough of Tower Hamlets, and was put towards the green and larger gardens and more amenities for the houses. Given that Montagu contributed such a large sum, it is surprising that none of the streets on the estate bear his name. The unusual road names are instead taken

from the names of earls or lords who once lived in the area. This cleverly makes a connection with Lordship Lane but omits Montagu (and the Lord Swaythling he was to become). However, the pre-war part of White Hart Lane became known as Tower Gardens because of the link with Tower Hamlets. It became a conservation area in 1978, though none of the houses is listed. Topham Square, added in the 1920s, was named after the lead architect of the interwar part of White Hart Lane, George Topham Forrest (1872–1945).

1

Source: Tjerk Ruimschotel (all pictures)

Old Oak Estate

Wulfstan Street,
Hammersmith and Fulham
*LCC Architects' Department/
Archibald Stuart Soutar*
1909–1914
⊖ East Acton

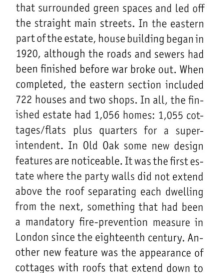

Old Oak Estate was the last project by the London County Council (LCC) Architects' Department before the First World War. For the project, the LCC bought 22 hectares of land, the purchase of which took from 1902 to 1905. During this time a strip of the land was sold to Great Western Railways and so the very precise plan for the estate of 1,527 cottages housing 11,438 people was altered. The estate was constructed in two phases: the first west of the railway (1911–1914) and the second east of the railway (1920–1923). The western section consisted of five shops and 333 cottages of varying sizes. Each home had a scullery and a bathroom. This part of Old Oak had a large number of terraces. The terraces were laid out in U-shapes that surrounded green spaces and led off the straight main streets. In the eastern part of the estate, house building began in 1920, although the roads and sewers had been finished before war broke out. When completed, the eastern section included 722 houses and two shops. In all, the finished estate had 1,056 homes: 1,055 cottages/flats plus quarters for a superintendent. In Old Oak some new design features are noticeable. It was the first estate where the party walls did not extend above the roof separating each dwelling from the next, something that had been a mandatory fire-prevention measure in London since the eighteenth century. Another new feature was the appearance of cottages with roofs that extend down to the top of the ground floor with dormer windows in the roofs for the bedrooms. The final design novelty was the use of the mock Tudor style in social housing. The style, also called Tudorbethan for its revival of aspects of Tudor and Elisabethan domestic architecture, later became common due to the lack of bricks following

the war: timber for roofing was available and so half-timbered façades were appealing in terms of cost as well as aesthetics. Archibald Stuart Soutar (1879–1951) was the LCC architect behind these features. He was the elder brother and collaborator of John Carrick Stuart Soutar (1881–1951), who supervised the design of homes in Hampstead Garden Suburb (010), which featured mock Tudor elements. The brothers likely worked together to implement the style in the two projects.

1

Interwar:
Estates

From 1915 to 1939

Progress Estate
Either side of Well Hall Road,
Greenwich
Office of Works/Frank Baines
1915
Eltham

016 A

The Progress Estate was designed as the period of Arts and Crafts-inspired architecture and town planning was coming to a close. As such, it is a late example of the picturesque tradition of the Garden City and Garden Suburb. Historically, it is significant as one of the earliest instances of state-funded social housing – in this case related to the production of weaponry at the nearby Woolwich Arsenal. On Friday 8 January 1915, the Ministry of Munitions, the Office of Works, and the Local Government Board agreed to construct over 1,000 houses for the estate, then named Well Hall. The board insisted that they be erected within six months, as there was an urgent need for housing for the arsenal's workers, and that the design was also to conform to the highest town-planning standards. The planning process took off at astonishing speed. On Saturday 9 January, Frank Baines (1877–1933), one of the three chief architects of the Office of Works, visited the site. Until 1911 Baines had been a temporary draughtsperson, but after that date, his career skyrocketed, and he was appointed chief architect of the Office of Works in January 1914. He did not have a lot of experience with residential buildings; he was mostly

known for his conservation and restoration work. On Sunday 10 January, four of Baines' colleagues with more experience in the field – J. A. Bowden, G. Parker, A. J. Pitcher, and G. E. Phillips – each came up with a different design for the site. The plan selected was by Phillips, who had not visited the area, but drew the layout of the streets to follow the curving contours of the land. After working through the night, Phillips finished the layout of the estate the next morning. A week later, the plans for the first 40 houses were done. Building work started on the farmland straddling Well Hall Road, where the Eltham to Woolwich tram service ran. The layout was carefully planned to look as if it had developed over time rather than being designed.

Houses were set back to retain the existing trees. Most of them had front gardens. The winding roads had green verges, and the street plan left space for two small public parks resembling traditional village greens. Faced with the wartime problems of shortages of building materials, the designers made use of any available resources. This practice resulted in a variety of finishes for the dwellings like brick, stone, slate, tile, timber-framing, and rendering. The variation in building forms further enhanced the picturesque appearance of the estate, sometimes referred to as 'the German village', which seems ironic given the underlying reasons for the development. Because the First World War made an ambitious timescale necessary, money was no issue. On 22 May 1915, the first block of houses was constructed, and two months later the estate was two-thirds complete. By August, the first houses were occupied. At the end of the year, 1,000 houses and 200 flats were finished. In half a year of building, completions were, at one point, at the rate of one house every two hours. In 1925 Progress Estates Ltd, a firm in which the Royal Arsenal Co-operative Society had a substantial interest, bought the estate. Since then the scheme has been known as the Progress Estate. The estate itself has been a conservation area since 1975, though none of the buildings is listed. In the 1990s, this idyllic garden suburb was the scene of one of the highest-profile racialist killings in the history of the UK. The way the police mishandled the case triggered profound cultural changes to attitudes towards racism and some legal and policing practices before two perpetrators were convicted almost 20 years late. On the evening of 22 April 1993, Stephen Lawrence, an 18-year-old black British youth, was murdered while waiting for a bus in Well Hall Road. In memory of the teenager, who was hoping to become an architect, the RIBA Stephen Lawrence Prize was set up by the Marco Goldschmied Foundation in 1998. The aim of this yearly award is to encourage emerging architectural talents working with budgets of under one million pounds sterling.

Dover House Estate

Straddles Dover House Road between Crestway and Upper Richmond Road, Wandsworth
LCC Architects' Department
1920–1927
🚆 Barnes

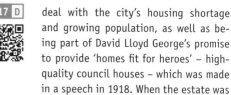
017 D

Dover House Estate was initially called Roehampton Estate, after the popular residential suburb in which it was situated. It was erected in the former grounds of the Dover and Putney manor houses. The former survived only in the name of the housing estate; the latter became a social centre, and was later sold off and subsequently converted into private flats. The estate was one of the first cottage estates constructed by London County Council (LCC) following the First World War. It formed part of the measures to deal with the city's housing shortage and growing population, as well as being part of David Lloyd George's promise to provide 'homes fit for heroes' – high-quality council houses – which was made in a speech in 1918. When the estate was completed in 1927, after seven years of building work, it contained 1,212 homes. These ranged from two-room flats to five-room houses and accommodated a total of 4,400 people. Since the estate housed, for the most part, the 'respectable' working class, such as public-transport workers, police officers, or Royal Mail employees, it was sometimes referred to as Uniform Town. The cottage-style homes are arranged in clusters around green spaces of varying sizes. The function of these spaces differed but was always communal and designed to generate a feeling of community: sometimes they were village

greens, sometimes recreation grounds or allotments. The biggest of them was the Pleasance, a large recreation ground. Allotments were originally provided in three areas behind the houses. Along with a school and a parade of shops on Upper Richmond Road, these were included to render the estate self-sufficient. The cottages also have their own open spaces: large gardens at the sides and front gardens with privet hedges. The site's existing trees were preserved in the layout for the estate, which features an orthogonal street pattern with garden-city features on either side of the straight Dover House Road. The individual homes either form part of a terrace or a semi-detached pair. The maximum amount of dwellings in a terrace is eighteen. They are always designed as one building with unifying features such as doors, windows, and porches, though these buildings each have their own identity. For instance, within the estate there are two types of roof: one is double-pitched, the other has eaves at first-floor level and dormer windows. These employ a range of materials, such as slate and clay tiles. Each building only has one type of roof, regardless of how many cottages are in it. The main material for the houses was London stock brick. The houses built in the first phase of construction of the estate all had metal casement windows, commonly known by the manufacturer's name, Crittall. The metal windows were expensive, and so timber was often used for sash windows in the later phases. The estate has changed over the years: one of the allotments was infilled by housing in the 1970s, the school was demolished, privet hedges have been replaced with other types of fences or walls.

Bellingham Estate
Bellingham, Lewisham
LCC Architects' Department/
George Topham Forrest
1920–1923
🖥 Bellingham

018 E

Bellingham Estate, in Lewisham, south London, was planned as a self-sufficient residential development to fill a triangular area between Southend Lane and two railway lines. Lewisham Council originally wanted to buy land in order to relocate people from the overpopulated areas of Deptford and Bermondsey. When Lewisham came up short, London County Council (LCC) purchased the land – at the time farmland – for one of their cottage estates. The building works for Bellingham lasted from 1920 to 1923. The estate has a Beaux-Arts-style formal plan and Garden Suburb housing types. LCC's chief architect

George Topham Forrest (1872–1945) placed the hexagonal Bellingham Green at its centre, onto which six tree-lined roads converge. Two churches were erected facing the green. The central axis, running from north to south, has a focal point in one of the two primary schools. Next to Bellingham Railway Station, facing a vast playing field, there are some shops and a pub. Pressure from the temperance movement made the LCC reluctant to accommodate pubs on its estates. When it was eventually decided that pubs were acceptable, they had to be designed along 'improved' lines with community facilities such as halls and games rooms, and referred to as 'refreshment houses'. The Fellowship Inn, with its mock Tudor stylings, appears to be one of the earliest such establishments built, and it is the only listed building (Grade II) on the estate. Bellingham is not a conservation area.

Source: Tjerk Ruimschotel (all pictures)

Downham Estate

Area either side of Downham Way, Bromley/Lewisham
LCC Architects' Department
1924–1930
🚉 Grove Park

019 E

The construction of Downham Estate – another of London County Council's (LCC) cottage estates – started in early 1924 and finished in summer 1930. The scheme is situated on an area of 210 hectares, of which 185 are in Lewisham and 25 are in Bromley. Five times as big as the first interwar LCC estate (Dover House [017]), it contains some 6,000 dwellings, although that is still only a fifth of the size of the largest LCC estate to be built during the interwar period (Becontree [020]). The construction was carried out by one of Britain's largest builders at the time, Holland, Hannen & Cubitts. For the most part, the homes at Downham were two-storey houses, ranging from five- to three-room dwellings. There were also around 400 flats contained in three-storey buildings. Both houses and flats were built from brick. Although the cottage estate is not as picturesque as other such developments – the houses do not feature the same Arts and Crafts detailing of previous estates – it does display some elements of Ebenezer Howard's garden city: the curved road layout and the handling of the open spaces. The areas unsuitable for housing were designated for parks and playing fields. At the southern edge of the estate, 13 hectares of land along Spring Brook became playing fields, as did some 8 hectares off Whitefoot Lane to the north. Next to the civic centre with its various shops, single public house, library and swimming pool, steep slopes provide open green spaces and wide views. The estate is

Source: Tjerk Ruimschotel (all pictures)

not a designated conservation area. However, it has a place in history because of its 2.5-metre-high brick wall, built across Valeswood Road in 1926. The wall was supposed to prevent Downham's 'undesirable' tenants from walking through a well-off owner-occupier estate to get to Bromley town centre. The wall stayed for some 25 years; people used other routes, and it became a fact of life.

Becontree Estate

Area between Ripple Road (A13) and Chadwell Heath Station, Barking and Dagenham
LCC Architects' Department
1921–1935
🚆 Chadwell Heath ⊖ Becontree

Located on an area of area of 1,200 hectares, Becontree was the largest of London County Council's out-county cottage estates. It occupies a plot of land 4 kilometres long and 3 kilometres wide. For the project, London County Council (LCC) selected 12,000 hectares of suitable land in the then-rural districts of Dagenham, Barking, and Ilford. Most of this vast area of land was covered by market gardens. LCC obtained it using compulsory purchase orders, with the aim of building 24,000 dwellings. The sheer size of Becontree necessitated a series of different districts with the appropriate amenities within it. The original plan placed civic and commercial facilities around Parsloes Park. But since the council did not hold much sway over the local authorities and commercial developments, this part of the plan was not implemented. Small rows of shops were built on the estate but there was no high street, and those living there had to go to Barking, Ilford, and, after 1937, Dagenham civic centre. According to Terence Young in a 1934 report for the Pilgrim Trust, this lack of amenities and community centres was detrimental to residents' quality of life in the fledgling estate. Since the planners did not expect Becontree's residents to own cars, the estate was devoid of car parks; they planned a tram line, which was never built. There were however rail stations nearby. Two schools were erected within the estate; the first opened in 1923 and the second in 1925. Green spaces and gardens provided areas for recreation, and the houses supplied their working-class tenants with the amenities of the time. There were more than 90 different types of houses, although all were quite similar and the variation encouraged in other cottage estates was largely absent. The homes were constructed in brick, a material that, unlike at the LCC's other estates,

were not easily available. They had to be shipped in by barge. An extensive jetty was erected over the River Thames and was capable of receiving seven barges at once. A light-rail line linked the pier to the Great Eastern Railway. The target number of houses was reached in 1934, and the ceremonial opening of Parsloes Park took place in July 1935. Christopher Addison, the member of parliament behind the Addison Act of 1919, an act that began a long tradition of council-house construction in the UK, cut the ribbon. Further homes were added in subsequent years – 800 in 1937, 600 from 1945 to 1951 in Heath Park, and later an extra 4,000. Apart from some houses from before the building of the estate and some garden walls, none of the buildings in Becontree is listed, and no part of the estate is a designated conservation area.

2

Watling Estate
Watling Avenue, Barnet
LCC Architects' Department/
George Topham Forrest
1927–1931
🚇 Burnt Oak

The Watling Estate was built to the designs of London County Council's (LCC's) chief architect George Topham Forrest (1872–1945) on a piece of land with an area of approximately 155 hectares. Construction work started in February 1926; in April 1927 the first residents moved in, and by 1931 all of the planned 4,000 dwellings were finished. Several building methods were employed: about half of the houses were built traditionally in brick, a third according to the Fidler system (concrete cast in-situ), 1 per cent in timber, and 5 per cent in steel using the Atholl system. The estate was designed as a garden suburb and was never meant to be self-sufficient. The land is gently undulating, leading up and away from the Burnt Oak Brook, which runs through the middle of the area. The lie of the land made it possible to create a distinctive layout based on garden-city design principles and to provide remarkable views from the roads into the internal open spaces – not a typical quality of social housing at the time.

Source: Tjerk Ruimschotel (all pictures)

The estate contains 8 hectares of parks and playing fields, and is served by several schools, medical centres, churches, and a library. Within its bounds, there are two shopping areas, namely Deansbrook Road in the north and at the southwestern edge Silkstream Parade along Watling Avenue. The German-born sociologist Ruth Durant (1912–1990), better known, after her second marriage, as Ruth Glass, studied the estate, and in 1939 she published *Watling: A Survey of Life on a New Housing Estate*. She was particularly interested in the way town planning related to community-building. Today approximately 45 per cent of the homes (3,600 houses and 400 flats) are rented social housing, 45 per cent are owner-occupied, and 10 per cent are privately rented. The Watling Estate is one of the few London County Council housing estates designated as a conservation area.

Kingsbury
Slough and Buck lanes, Brent
Ernest Trobridge
1920–1940
Ⓣ Kingsbury

Slough and Buck lanes in the district of Kingsbury, northwest London, are the sites of the best surviving examples of the dwellings designed and built by the eccentric architect-cum-developer Ernest Trobridge. Born in 1884 in Belfast, he trained there as an architect. After winning a scholarship, he moved to London in the late 1900s. Trobridge was a devout member of the New Church and so attempted to incorporate the theories of the Swedish philosopher and theologian Emanuel Swedenborg (1688–1772) into his designs. His houses display a mixture of Swedenborgian symbolism and functional features: sheltering thatched roofs, brick fireplaces as focal points, and elaborate entrances. Such elements were coupled with his patented 'compressed green wood' construction system, a method that made use of elm – cheap and plentiful at the time – which was cut and shaped while still green. The system, which incorporated adjustments for shrinkage, produced lightweight and strong homes. Houses could be built in just eight weeks. They were designed to be not only quick and affordable, but also to provide accommodation and employment (via their construction) for the servicemen returning from the First World War. In 1920, Trobridge showed a pair of semi-detached model houses at London's Ideal Home Exhibition. Following their success, he then built two timber estates. From 1920 to 1922 he worked on the Ferndene Estate, on the corner of Slough Lane and Kingsbury Road. It was planned as 32 homes in groups of four. However, after disputes with the local council, only ten detached houses were built, including his own: Hayland at 156 Slough Lane (1921). Since the project was a financial disaster, a wealthy fellow church member helped

out with the funds for the second estate: Elmwood (1922–1924). Again, the project was scaled back. Only one group of four homes from this development still stands today: 345–351 Stag Lane (1922). After working on the two estates, he widened his range of materials and designed for individual clients and small developers. These projects can be seen at 89–107 Colindeep Lane, 25–31 the Loning, Hayland Close (3, 12, 15–16, 19), and Buck Lane (3–5, 15, 17, 19, 21, 37, 53, 54). In the early 1930s, Trobridge helped establish the Kingsbury Cross Co-Partnership, a project to develop an estate of homes for people with low incomes to buy or rent. For this, he designed all the dwellings in Oak Tree Dell and Ash Tree Dell (parallel cul-de-sacs off Buck Lane). The middle of that decade saw his most elaborate buildings: several castle-like apartment blocks at the point where Buck Lane crosses Wakeman's Hill Avenue/Highfield Avenue. These buildings feature a host of unusual elements: turrets,

Source: Tjerk Ruimschotel (all pictures)

elaborate chimneys, coal hatches. They are: Whitecastle Mansions (1935, 9 flats), Rochester Court (1935, 16 flats), Highford Court (1935–1936, 4 flats) and Tudor Gates (1934–1936, 8 maisonettes). He also built some three-storey blocks around Highfield Avenue: Shirley Court (1937, 12 flats) and Mountaire Court (1936–1938, 30 flats). The latter was Trobridge's last built work. He died in 1942, at the age of 58 from diabetes: because of his vegetarian beliefs, he refused insulin, which at that time was extracted from animal pancreases.

2

Source: Tjerk Ruimschotel (all pictures)

Hanger Hill Garden Estate

Princes Gardens, Ealing
Douglas Smith & Barley
1928–1936

023 A

West Acton

The Hanger Hill Garden Estate is a remarkable instance of a commercial development in a style that is generally disparaged by architects but favoured by clients: mock Tudor. Such half-timbered homes were favoured by buyers in the late 1920s and the 1930s and remain so nowadays. This development of more than 600 units was built to a design by the firm Douglas Smith & Barley. It was erected on land that formerly accommodated an aerodrome and factory. The works took place in two phases. The first (1928–1932) was situated on the eastern side of Acton Boundary Stream (once a border between Acton and Ealing) and included Princes Gardens, Tudor Gardens, Vale Lane, and some of Monks and Queens drives. The second (1933–1936) was located on the western side of the stream and completed the layout of the estate. A section of the stream can still be seen behind the houses in Garage Road. During the construction period of the estate, a community feel arose, facilitated by the sheltered atmosphere and the landscaped environment. The surroundings include a rose garden and a 'village' pond. Hanger Hill Gardens contains 258 flats in blocks along Queens Drive, Links Road, and Monks Drive. These apartment blocks take the appearance of freestanding Tudor manor houses set in spacious lawns. The estate's 361 houses are semi-detached or in short terraces and are built according to prototypes which generated variety within the overall design. After the Second World War, the damaged houses at 41–47 Princes Gardens were rebuilt; however, due to the shortages of materials, the external Tudor timbers were omitted. Until the 1950s all the dwellings were rented out. In 1954 houses in the eastern part were sold individually; those in the western part went on sale from 1969. The estate was declared a conservation area in 1969.

Hanger Hill

Off Hanger Green, Ealing
Welch, Cachemaille-Day & Lander
1931

🚇 Park Royal

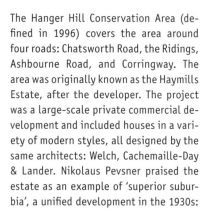

The Hanger Hill Conservation Area (defined in 1996) covers the area around four roads: Chatsworth Road, the Ridings, Ashbourne Road, and Corringway. The area was originally known as the Haymills Estate, after the developer. The project was a large-scale private commercial development and included houses in a variety of modern styles, all designed by the same architects: Welch, Cachemaille-Day & Lander. Nikolaus Pevsner praised the estate as an example of 'superior suburbia', a unified development in the 1930s:

in contrast to other estates triggered by the building of public transport stations, here the architects of the estate also designed the commercial centre (in the Hanger Green area) and the tube station (Park Royal). The crescent-shaped commercial centre adjacent to Western Avenue contains shops, offices, flats, a hotel, and a garage. There the architects sought to escape from a cosy garden-city image but did not apply an overly harsh modernist language. The layout of the development consists of three semi-circular roads, arranged concentrically (Chatsworth Road, the Ridings, Ashbourne Road), with Corringway defining the southern and eastern boundaries. Beaufort and Audley roads run inside Corringway, crossing the Ridings and

Source: Tjerk Ruimschotel (all pictures)

Ashbourne Road. All of the streets more or less follow the contours of Hanger Hill. The lines of the streets give continuously varied perspectives of the estate, and the sloping terrain provides views over the surrounding landscape. The houses themselves are also diverse: there are four main types, each with multiple variants; the types are spread throughout the estate. An Ealing Council conservation report from 2008 lists the main types as mock Tudor and neo-Georgian (the two most common on the estate), as well as Modern Movement (classic modernist buildings with flat roofs, strip windows and so on); mostly seen along the Ridings) and Moderne (ordinary houses sprinkled with modernist elements such as metal windows and horizontal banding).

Throughout the estate, the homes are individual, yet viewed together they project a harmonious impression. Most of the houses in the southern part of the estate were completed before the outbreak of the Second World War. The post-war shortage of building materials resulted in simplified designs for the northern part.

2

Elm Park Garden City
The Broadway, Havering
Costain
1935–1939
Elm Park

025 A

In 1933 the Liverpool-based developer Richard Costain Ltd planned Elm Park: a garden city for 35,000 people, living in 7,000 dwellings, on an area of 240 hectares. The development, advertised at the time as 'the complete country hometown', was to have eight schools, five shopping centres, two churches, an inn, and a park. Costain capitalised on the opening of the Ford factory in nearby Dagenham in 1931, where workers wanted to live close to the plant. The District Line had been extended to Upminster in 1932, and Costain also helped finance the estate's new tube station. After just 500 houses had been erected, both Elm Park Garden City and the tube station were opened in May 1935. The ceremony was conducted by the Minister of Health, Hilton Young – a sign of both the significance of the project and the connections possessed by the Costain family business. The majority of funding for Elm Park came from the Halifax Building Society, whose president wanted to help the working class move from cramped inner-city rented accommodation to spacious owner-occupied houses in the suburbs. Home buyers could choose from a variety of house types, with romantic names such as Coronation Arcadia, Villette, Havenwood and Hawthorne. Some were erected as show homes close to the estate office. A distinctive feature of the estate's first houses was the large family kitchen, one outcome of Costain's market-research findings. From the start, a local social life was promoted through the residents' association, sports clubs, and assembly hall. By 1939 there were 2,600 houses and a commercial high street leading to the station. The Second World War put a stop to building works. Construction was taken over by the local council after the end of the war, and continued into the 1960s.

Source: Tjerk Ruimschotel (all pictures)

Gidea Park

026 A

Between Eastern Avenue and
Gidea Park Station, and between
Rafael Park and Romford Golf
Course, Havering
Various architects
1934
🚊 Gidea Park

Gidea Park in east London twice served as the site for a 'housing exhibition' – something that has not happened often in Britain. These shows – the first in 1911 and the second in 1934 – both displayed modest suburban houses. In the first, the homes were designed by leading figures of the late Arts and Crafts Movement and in the second by architects involved in the early Modern Movement. The first was more successful than the second in terms of winning over the public; it demonstrated the charm of relatively small houses and cottages set in a garden suburb environment. The second is more remarkable as an experiment. Romford Garden Suburb, as Gidea Park used to be called, was constructed around 1910 on the grounds of the Gidea Hall and Balgores estates. More than 100 architects submitted over 150 plans for small homes for the suburb-cum-exhibition. Well-known figures included Parker & Unwin, Baillie Scott, and Clough Williams-Ellis. The best plans were built within half a year; six of them are now Grade II listed. These

houses demonstrated that affordable yet high-quality suburban housing could be created, and they could be purchased. In the period leading up to the mid-1920s, 100 houses in similar styles were erected in the suburb. The Modern Homes competition and exhibition of 1934 generated more entries – almost 500 – and 35 houses, 20 of which were semi-detached, were built that same year in the north-eastern corner of the existing suburb. This exhibition was different from the first in that the homes were primarily show houses (although they could be bought) and that the aim was to sell some 300 plots on which homes similar to the winning entries could be built. There were 25 winning designs, five from each of the classes, which ranged from A (the least expensive) to E (the most expensive). Among these there were examples of various architectural languages, including the International Style, Moderne, and other interwar styles that blended contemporary and traditional English house forms. However, the majority of the 150 houses subsequently constructed along Eastern and Link avenues and other areas of the estate were not in a modernist style. Today only a few examples of the winning designs survive, and they are grouped according to class. The five Class E houses are situated on Heath Drive, facing Romford Golf Course. House number 60 is a modernist design by Scott, Chesterton & Shepherd (who built

in all but one class). Numbers 61, 62 and 63 were designed with sloping roofs and are often not recognised as being part of the exhibition. Of the Class E designs, all but one had four bedrooms, all have garages and kitchen doors – sometimes explicitly designated for trades – and some mention servants' toilets or rooms. The Class D houses are the first five at the uneven side of Brook Road; all have their own garage and some a roof terrace, sun terrace, or sleeping balcony. Interrupted by a traditional house, the row of exhibition houses continues with Class C dwellings at numbers 13, 15, and 17 (with sloping roof), and 18 and 20 across the street. Class A and B houses are semi-detached and have no garage. They were all built along Eastern Avenue, starting, just around the corner from Heath Drive, with five pairs of B homes and – after a conventional four-apartment semi – the remaining five houses of Class A. The last two pairs have sloping roofs but were clearly part of the exhibition. The rather small A and B houses have been expanded and

Gidea Park: Modernist flat-roofed detached houses in Brook Road, dating from the 1934 Modern Homes exhibition and competition .

modified by their inhabitants in a manner resembling Le Corbusier's homes in Pessac, France, before restoration. The most famous modernist house originating from the exhibition is 64 Heath Drive by Francis Skinner (1908–1998), a member of the by radical firm Tecton. He was only 25 when he designed it. The house is constructed of reinforced concrete and set in an L-plan, with a roof terrace on the first floor, adjacent to the three bedrooms. The design for this one-off could be used in series to produce a terrace of dwellings with semi-patio gardens behind a long communal white wall. It won first prize in its class. The building was Grade II listed in 1997 and has since been restored. There is a noteworthy, though unlisted, pair of modernist semi-detached Class A houses at 320 and 322 Eastern Avenue. These were designed by Holford, Stevenson & Yorke – Yorke being F. R. S. Yorke (1906–1962), an influential architect who was a founder member of the firm YRM and the author of *The Modern House* (1934) and *The Modern House in England* (1937).

2

Wells Rise
1, 3, 4–10 Wells Rise,
Westminster
Burnet, Tait & Lorne
1934
St John's Wood

027 B

This short street off Regent's Park is perhaps the only place in London where one can envision what a modernist street of the 1930s might have looked like. The houses, located on both sides of the street, were commissioned in 1934 by Freda Dudley Ward and her future husband, the Marques de Casa Maury. Although the houses were designed by Burnet, Tait & Lorne, one of the most important British architectural firms of the interwar period, they are relatively little known and poorly documented. It is unclear which architect from the practice drew the design. In any case, the commission was won by Francis Lorne, an architect of Scottish origin who, after 16 years working in America, joined Burnet & Tait. On the side of the street with odd numbering, there is the shortest terrace possible – two non-mirrored houses – while on the other side there are four terraced houses (numbers 4 to 10). The slope of the street is echoed in the staggered roofline. The individual houses have a two-storey-high staircase window. The awning above the front door continues to the canopy above the garage door of the adjoining house. Only numbers 1, 3, and 4 still have the original garages. The homes have been adjusted somewhat over the years, but with relatively little damage to the Modern feel. The houses are not listed; the letterbox on the corner with Prince Albert Road is.

Source: Bob Bronshoff (all pictures)

Genesta Road

85–91 Genesta Road,
Greenwich
Berthold Lubetkin
1935

⊖ Woolwich Arsenal

2

Berthold Lubetkin was born in Tbilisi, Georgia, in 1901. He studied architecture in Warsaw and Paris and immigrated to England in 1931. A year later, he partnered with a group of six Architectural Association graduates and formed the radical practice Tecton. Outside this group, Lubetkin worked on a scheme for this terrace of four town houses on Genesta Road. The commission from George West Ltd was secured by another European émigré Anton Vivian Pilichovsky (1907–1982; later called Vivien Pilley). But the authorship of the design is Lubetkin's alone. His quartet of homes is arranged in two mirrored pairs and implanted in the middle of a nineteenth-century terraced street. Modernist architects tended to overlook the traditional terraced house, but here Lubetkin succeeded in achieving a modern interpretation of it: the project oscillates between a bespoke design for a single house and a sort of modernist prêt-à-porter version of an English rowhouse. Because of the topography of the site, other homes on the street have their entrances at first-floor level. Lubetkin, however, set the entrances on the ground floor – almost a storey below street level – and planned spiral staircases to access the other floors. The first floors contain the reception rooms and kitchens and the second floors the three bedrooms and the bathrooms. This arrangement gives the full length of the 6-metre-long frontage to the living room and provides off-street parking next to the front door. The design is one of the first to deal with the problem of the private car and one of the few to come up with a sound solution, though the space is a little tight for today's vehicles. There are two parallel paths, one for pedestrians and one for the car, changing the space in front of the building from a purely pedestrian domain into one that is more connected to the road. The frontage and the side retaining walls with planting boxes, gate posts and gates are an important part of the composition. Unfortunately, Lubetkin did not accept the invitation of C. J. Pell & Co., the contractor of this project, to become the firm's in-house architect for similar developments. It would have been very interesting to see this Grade II*-listed housing project scaled up to form a whole street or even perhaps a neighbourhood.

Source: Bob Bronshoff (all pictures)

Frognal Close
1-6 Frognal Close, Camden
Ernst L. Freud
1937
� Finchley Road & Frognal
🚇 Hampstead

029 B

Frognal Close is a fine example of the modernist interwar architecture aimed at a middle- and upper-middle-class clientele. The ensemble is made up of six semi-detached houses arranged along a private cul-de-sac that widens out to form a square. It comprises two mirrored pairs on each side (listed Grade II) and a pair at the end where the cul-de-sac joins the main road. The end pair of houses have garages attached while the other pairs have their garages on the square. This was not Ernst L. Freud's original design, which envisaged two detached houses and two semis on the end. He had to adapt his idea to meet planning regulations. The Austrian architect (son

of the psychoanalyst Sigmund Freud) had studied in Vienna and Berlin, and then in 1933, banned from practising in Germany, had left for London. For the most part, his work in England consisted of designing private houses and blocks of flats around Hampstead. Another good example of his work is Belvedere Court (1937–1938), an art-deco-style block of 56 flats in nearby East Finchley, constructed to house Jewish families fleeing Nazi Germany.

Source: Tjerk Ruimschotel (all pictures)

Willow Road
1–3 Willow Road, Camden
Ernö Goldfinger, 1939
🚉 Hampstead Heath
🚇 Hampstead

`030` `B`

Willow Road is a modernist interpretation of the traditional Georgian terrace: it incorporates contemporary materials and a free-plan approach more suited to a detached villa than to a series of houses. Its architect, Ernö Goldfinger (1902–1987), saw it as a prototype for urban row-housing and published drawings showing how it could be adapted for streets and squares. However, he also had personal reasons for designing it: to house his family (house number 2 became their home), to invest some of his wife's capital (she had inherited the Crosse & Blackwell company in the early 1930s), and to display his architectural skill. The trio of flat-roofed houses is three storeys high at the front and four storeys at the back, partly due to the topography of the site. The floors are supported by reinforced-concrete columns and three cylindrical drums that each contain a cantilevered spiral staircase (arranged in a horizontal line across the middle of the house). The external walls are faced in red brick. The front façade reveals the three separate storeys. The ground floor has three recessed entrances and four garage doors; the garages of houses 1 and 3 support the first-floor balconies. On the first floor, a long continuous window with two concrete frames runs almost the entire length of the three dwellings. French windows provide access to the balconies in houses 1 and 3. On the second floor, the seven individual windows show nothing of the three different houses or the six separate bedrooms behind them. The master bedroom in number 2, the middle house, is the only room with two windows. This larger middle house has a floor area of 300 m² and two garages, while the other two houses each

have an area of 200 m² and a garage. The two end houses have a simpler layout than the middle one: a kitchen and dining room on the ground floor, an L-shaped living room and a master bedroom on the first floor, and four bedrooms on the second floor. The spiral staircases, placed near the party walls, connect all levels, including the basement. The middle house – Goldfinger's residence – is symmetrically organised around the staircase. The ground floor contains the kitchen and the servant's quarters at the back and the garages and an entrance area between them (the entrance area was originally supposed to include a separate door for tradespeople, but this was removed during the final stages of the design). At the rear of the first floor, overlooking the back garden, is a living room and study with built-in bookcases and a curved frame for exhibiting paintings over the fireplace. Across the front of the house are the architect's studio and a dining room, with bespoke furniture designed by Goldfinger. A kitchenette was added in the 1960s. The second floor contains the master bedroom and its en suite at the front, and a guest room with a tip-up bed and a washbasin concealed in a cupboard. Along the rear façade were more three bedrooms (two for the children, one for a nanny). With movable walls and a foldaway bed for the nanny, this area could serve as a nursery during the day. Later, after the children left home, Goldfinger's mother moved into this part of the house, and the ground floor and basement were remodelled as a separate flat for the family of one of his sons. Thus, at one time, four generations of the same family lived in the house. Goldfinger lived there for almost 50 years, continually changing and adapting the house to his requirements. Today, the house still contains the furniture, artworks and contents of its former owners. It is a Grade II* listed National Trust property and is open to the public.

Interwar:
Blocks and Buildings

From 1915 to 1939

Ossulston Estate

031 B

Between Ossulston Street
and Chalton Street, Camden
LCC Architects' Department/
George Topham Forrest et al.
1927–1931
🚆🚇 Euston

Although it had a policy of constructing out-county cottage estates in the early twentieth century, London County Council (LCC) built this inner-city estate with the aim of alleviating some pressing issues of the day: long waiting lists for housing and the appalling slum conditions in the area. The Ossulston Estate was erected on the site of a former slum. It occupies a long and thin plot, around 400 metres long and 75 metres wide, covering 3.5 hectares. The LCC's lead architect on the project was George Topham Forrest (1872–1945) and the assistants Reginald Minton Taylor and E. H. Parks. In 1924 he had visited the USA to study the construction of high-rise buildings. In this context, he conceived four closed urban blocks and a U-shaped block attached to an existing church and school (both later demolished) for Ossulston in 1925. To deal with the demand for affordable dwellings on a limited site, he originally proposed nine-storey blocks. The design contained shops on the ground floor, offices on the first floor, two floors of 'flats of character superior to the ordinary working-class dwellings', and then working-class flats on the upper five floors. The two classes of dwellings would have separate entrances, staircases, and lifts. This was the first design for high-rise housing for working-class tenants in London. Although not quite rejected, this initial scheme later had to make way for a different sort of urban planning – one likely influenced by Forrest's visit to the Karl-Marx-Hof in Vienna (Karl Ehn, 1927–1930) in 1927. Forrest envisaged an elaborate mix of three- to seven-storey courtyard blocks and lower street-front buildings, and two nine-storey high-rises: one in the courtyard of the northernmost block for working-class tenants (Walker House) and the other for middle-class tenants as

Interwar: Blocks and Buildings

part of a completely redrawn southern section (Levita House). The latter consisted of two square buildings with courtyards, connected to the high-rise block by four diagonal buildings. During the construction of the first three blocks of flats around a courtyard (Chamberlain House, 1927–1929), the design for Walker House lost its central high-rise and two-deck garage. The main part of Walker House was erected from 1929 to 1930: it became a five-storey building surrounding a courtyard with no access from the surrounding streets. The brick sections were added in 1937. Both Walker and Chamberlain houses contain shops and pubs at

Ossulston Estate: Northern courtyard of Levita House

ground-floor level along Phoenix Road. The homes are accessed not via the street but through the courtyards. Levita House was built from 1930 to 1935. Its height was reduced from that stipulated in the original plans – the blocks ended up ranging from three- to six-storeys in height – though its bold, winged shape was still dramatic. There was no lift and all the flats were for working-class tenants. The Ossulston Estate is one of the few examples of the interaction between modernist housing in Europe and British council housing in the interwar period. It was particularly innovative in terms of layout. The estate is currently Grade II listed.

Grosvenor Estate
Page Street, Westminster
Edwin Lutyens
1930
⊖ Pimlico

032 D

At the time the Grosvenor Estate was commissioned, Edwin Lutyens (1869–1944) was already a renowned architect: he had received gold medals from the Royal Institute of British Architects (1921) and the American Institute for Architects (1925) and was known for his war memorials and his mansions for rich clients. He was therefore perhaps an odd choice for a social-housing project to replace an existing slum. His connection to Detmar Blow, the real-estate manager to the Second Duke of Westminster – the owner of the land on which the Grosvenor Estate was built – helped him obtain first a job working on the Duke's own Grosvenor House and then the commission for Grosvenor Estate (then known as the Page Street Estate to avoid confusion with the Duke's property). For the project, Lutyens deviated from his usual classically-inspired design, introducing striking chequerboard façades of stock brick and white rendering. However, the detailing on the gates, pavilions, and gate piers reveals that he had not fully departed from his normal style. The housing estate, just north of the Millbank Estate (London County Council Architects Department [012]), consists of seven buildings: three on the north side of Page Street, two south of Page Street (between Page and Vincent streets), and two south of Vincent Street. The main streets pre-date the estate and together with the available land formed the framework that dictated the number and size of the buildings. All of the buildings are

U-shaped. The trio of buildings – Abady, Edric, and Bennett houses – wrap around paved courtyards that open onto Page Street. Each of these six-storey-high buildings contains 80 flats. Inside the U-shapes there are wide access galleries. Between these three blocks, two partly paved playgrounds were created. Along Page Street, there are three freestanding pavilions situated at the open ends of the playgrounds and inside the U of Edric House. Abady and Bennett houses each have a smaller pavilion attached to them, closing off the gated courtyards. These single-storey neo-Georgian-style buildings serve as gatehouses. The two buildings between Page and Vincent streets – Rogers and Tothill houses – are the largest on the estate. Their U-shapes turn their backs on Page Street and open on to Vincent Street. These blocks are five storeys high and overlook a communal

garden/playground, which was created after parts of these two buildings were removed in the 1970s. With this change, the total number of dwellings on the estate was reduced to 592. The two narrow blocks south of Vincent Street – Duke and Princess Mary houses – take a shortened U form. They contain 35 flats each. Why Duke and Princess Mary houses were Grade II listed in 1987 and the other blocks of this coherent estate only three years later is unclear. The estate and four unlisted red-brick blocks west of it (Schomberg House by Ashley & Newman, 1927; and Jessel, Probyn, and Norfolk houses), were designated a conservation area in 2010. It is worth mentioning that, during the 1990s, Grosvenor was one of the estates where the notorious Building Stable Communities policy was to be implemented. Contrary to the term 'stable', the semi-secret objective of this scheme was to alter the neighbourhoods by selling off council housing. The intention was to replace tenants – who were thought to be more likely to vote Labour – with owner-occupants – who were supposed to be more likely to vote Conservative. This illegal policy, described as 'homes for votes', was targeted at electoral wards where the Conservative city council could lose its majority in the 1990 elections. The policy was eventually stopped, but in the case of the Grosvenor Estate, Gerald Grosvenor, the sixth Duke of Westminster – the owner of the land on which the estate was built, since the second Duke of Westminster had granted the local authorities a 999-year lease – wanted the housing to remain accessible to those on low incomes. In the end, the Duke went to court to prevent Westminster City Council from selling the estate. In this Westminster versus Westminster case, the court found in the Duke's favour.

3

Cholmeley Lodge
1–48 Cholmeley Park, Haringey
Guy Morgan
1935
⊖ Archway

033 B

This six-storey mansion block responds well to its site: along Cholmeley Park, perpendicular to the main road and near the top of Highgate Hill. This is particularly remarkable because its architect, Guy Morgan (1902–1987), initially designed the building for a seafront site in Bournemouth. However, the seaside town rejected its modern appearance in favour of a gentler look. Morgan, who until 1927 had worked in the office of Edwin Lutyens, reused the design for the more forward-thinking environment of Highgate Village. His style can be compared with the nearby High Point I, which was being built around the same time: instead of a more European version of the International Style, with smooth white elevations, Morgan took up an art deco language, designing a sweeping main façade with stripes of brick interspersed with lines of windows divided by cast-stone panels. Each of the four doorways is set

under its own rounded canopy, atop which there are letters spelling out Cholmeley Lodge in a typical 1930s typeface. Inside, there are 4 two-bedroom and 4 three-bedroom apartments per floor. The building features six different apartment types, with the apartments at ground-floor level modified to make room for the entrances. The flat roof of the block was intended as a sun deck. Cholmeley Lodge shares its art deco style with what is likely Morgan's best-known building: Florin Court, the mansion block used as the home of Agatha Christie's character Hercule Poirot in the television series *Poirot*.

3

Du Cane Court
Balham High Road, Wandsworth
G. Kay Green
1937
🚇 Balham

034 D

Although it is not currently a listed building, Du Cane Court is nevertheless a milestone in art deco architecture. When it opened in 1937, it contained 676 apartments and so was likely the largest block of privately-owned flats in Europe (though the feat was quickly surpassed by Dolphin Square, a residential building designed by Costain, containing over 1,300 units). It included innovative features for the time: central heating, constant hot water, telephone booths and letterboxes on every floor, pre-installed wiring for individual phones, and a radio with a choice of two programmes. Some apartments in the first section of the building had rubbish chutes. Communal amenities for the residents included a shop and a large restaurant on the seventh floor, where regular dinner dances were held (the restaurant was later converted into more flats). The estate was erected in two stages. In the first stage, blocks the shape of a capital 'E' were built near Balham High Road. This 'E' opens onto the road but is set back from it. During the second stage blocks with the same footprint were constructed directly behind the first 'E'. This created a total of ten blocks, arranged around four courtyards. The apartments ranged from two bedsits sharing a bathroom to three-bedroom flats with separate dining room. There were also two- and three-bedroom maisonettes. The maisonettes had private access from street level, while the apartments were reached via an internal corridor. The flats at the ends of each street-facing wing had their own entrance halls and lifts, while at the centre of the building there was an impressive entrance lobby. The Scottish architect George Kay Green (1877–1939) specialised in designing large-scale housing blocks in the 1930s. His other works include Sloane Avenue Mansions (1933) and Nell Gwynn House (1937), both in Chelsea. There are various rumours surrounding the building's history during the Second World War: that it remained untouched by bombs as the Nazis used it as a landmark for navigation and had placed spies in it. It was even believed that Hitler had earmarked the building (like Senate House of the University of London) as his headquarters in the event of a successful invasion. This urban myth was enhanced by the fact that, although the floor plan of Du Cane House does not resemble a swastika, it could easily be turned into one by erasing three blocks and introducing one.

Source: Philipp Meuser (all pictures)

Pullman Court

Streatham Hill, Lambeth
Frederick Gibberd
1935
🚇 Streatham Hill

This modernist masterpiece marked the extraordinary start of the career of Frederick Gibberd (1908–1984), an English architect and urban planner who specialised in designing flats and later created the master plan for Harlow New Town. He was also the architect of Heathrow Airport (1950–1970) and Liverpool Metropolitan Cathedral (1967). In 1937 Gibberd co-authored (with F. R. S. Yorke) *The Modern Flat*, a book about the new residential architecture of the interwar period. Pullman Court was designed as 'the place to be' for young professionals; it was a new and exciting alternative to the dreary lodging houses of the time. When Gibberd was just 23 years old and a year out of university, he met the secretary of the developer William Bernstein.

Through that chance meeting, he met Bernstein, who said he would provide the funding for flats for single persons if Gibberd could find a site. That site was the former location of a children's home, atop a hill in south London. Gibberd's original plan, based on the novel concept of small flats for singles, was modified to include housing for couples and small families in order to counter the fear of others in the neighbourhood that such a residential complex would lead to promiscuity. He described the ensemble of blocks of different heights and housing typologies as 'one-, two- and three-room flats for bachelors, married couples, office workers.' There were 218 flats in various blocks: five three-storey blocks (types A and C), each with two three-room flats per floor; two T-shaped five-storey blocks with galleries for access (type B), each with six one-room flats and six two-room flats per floor; and two seven-storey blocks (type D), each with five three-room flats per floor. There were variations in this

3

layout at ground-floor level. The one-room studios measured a little over 20 m². A one-bedroom (two-room) flat would be twice as large, with a walnut sliding partition between the bedroom and living room and a private balcony with views over communal gardens, also twice as big as a one-room balcony. None of the ground-floor apartments has a private outdoor space; the landscaped garden extends to the walls of the buildings. Because of the compact size of the flats, Gibberd specially designed furniture that tenants could buy. All flats had built-in kitchens, closets and cupboards and state-of-the-art Crittall windows. Communal amenities included central heating, sun terraces on the roofs, social rooms, a doctor's surgery, lock-up garages, pram and bicycle storage, and an outdoor swimming pool (now filled in). The various residential building types are organised around two semi-enclosed courtyards, linked along the long axis of the long narrow site. The complex has a near symmetrical composition, save that the two T-shaped blocks (B), which run parallel, are not mirrored. The living rooms and balconies in both blocks face south, leaving the north side for the long slabs for access galleries. The road between these blocks is for both vehicle traffic and pedestrians. At the western perimeter of the estate, the ensemble is set back from the street. Either side of the entrance, three-storey blocks (A) are

placed in line with the height of the existing buildings. Because of the oblique southern boundary of the building plot, there was only room for one block (C) projecting from the entrance block towards the main road. Abutting the short section of the T-shaped blocks, two five-storey blocks (C) connect with the seven-storey towers to partly enclose the main courtyard. The buildings have reinforced concrete frames and the exterior walls are made of 10-centimetre-thick reinforced concrete. These were poured with fibreboard for a smooth finish and lined with 2.5-centimetre-thick cork for insulation. Although Pullman Court is famous for being a white 1930s ensemble, some of its exterior walls were originally painted in pastel colours, as analyses of paint samples by the Architectural Paint Research Unit of English Heritage showed in the 1990s. The architect himself stipulated the colour palette as 'warm browns and beige and cool white and blue at the rear.' The walls were supposed to be repainted every five years, and to facilitate this without periodic erection of scaffolding, rolled steel beams for suspended work platforms were installed along the roofline. The original colours have been reintroduced in several places in recent renovations. Pullman Court was listed Grade II in 1981, and after extensive repairs to the exterior, its listing status was raised to Grade II* in 1997.

Highpoint I & II
High Hill, Haringey
Berthold Lubetkin
1935–1938
⊖ Highgate

The two Highpoint buildings, designed by Berthold Lubetkin and Tecton, demonstrate the possibilities that modernism offered for new housing in the 1930s: new layouts, construction techniques, and aesthetics. Situated in a leafy suburban context, they verge on being unassuming. However, the fact that they were listed Grade I as early as 1974 betrays their importance as landmarks in early British modernism. The brief for Highpoint I was to develop a building to house the employees of Gestetner, an office equipment manufacturer. But when a suitable site in prosperous Highgate was found, the scheme was adapted to allow private tenancies. When Lubetkin put pressure on Gestetner to let the flats to mixed social groups, a few local residents moved into the low-rent flats, although they often felt uncomfortable beside the professionals living at the prestigious address. The building itself has a double-cruciform plan and is set at an angle to the road. It is seven storeys high and its garden at the back slopes down due to the topography of the site. Larger flats are placed at right angles to the main spine and have long balconies on the eastern and western sides. The end flats have short balconies with double curved fronts. Square glazed windows serve the utility areas. Originally there were four three-bedroom and four two-bedroom apartments on each upper floor. The street-facing section of the ground floor contained one three-bedroom flat (which according to the designs 'could be converted to a snack bar in case of need'), two studios, and a porter's flat, and the rear section contained three flats: two three-bedroom and one two-bedroom. The lower ground floor comprised two studios and 16 maid's rooms (now two flats). Inspired by Le Corbusier, Lubetkin designed the route to the apartments as a promenade architecturale. A curved driveway leads between the pilotis under the cantilevered porch. The main

entrance opens into the free-shaped lobby. From there, a flight of stairs leads to the long hallway under the central spine of the block. At both ends are cores with lifts and stairs to the apartments. Beyond the western core is a tearoom opening to the garden with tennis courts. The design and building of Highpoint I incorporated many innovative features. As an alternative to a normal concrete framework, the designers and engineers chose a system using sliding formwork and removable platforms rather than scaffolding. The resulting structure of monolithic walls and floors had no problem with poor joints. However, the walls later turned out to be too thin and required frequent maintenance and repair. To conceal the concrete beam supporting the middle of the floor slab, Tecton even designed built-in cabinets and wardrobes. The long horizontal steel windows of the living rooms have a bespoke 'concertina' opening method, sliding along metal rails. Other innovations included radiator panels fixed to the ceiling and built-in refrigerators that had a central condenser in the basement. Next to the residents' lift, a separate system of small service elevators gave access to carefully designed kitchen areas.

Shortly after Highpoint I was finished, the neighbouring parcel of land to the south became available. Lubetkin convinced Gestetner to purchase the land and build more middle-class housing in line with Highpoint I. Highgate residents, united in the Highgate Preservation Committee, opposed another large block of what they saw as working-class housing in their neighbourhood and specified that 'any future buildings had to preserve the architectural character of the area'. During the long design process, many different options were proposed, and in the end the building volume was limited to one six-storey block as an extension of one of Highpoint I's 'arms'. To deal with the reduced volume and the rising costs, the brief for Highpoint II was changed from 57 flats to 12 luxury apartments. This second Highpoint building is remarkable in that it stretches the visual vocabulary of modernism beyond that of the classic white concrete box. Although Highpoint II had to be simpler in shape, its materials and floor plan could be more elaborate than the first tower. This high-end building presented the box framing with brick and tile infill that Lubetkin, Tecton, and others later employed in low-cost housing. It contained six four-bedroom maisonettes in the centre. These have double-height living rooms – a feature of modern luxury flats at the time – and an oval stairway giving onto an open landing. Around the centre are six smaller four-bedroom maisonettes. At the entrance, two casts of the Erechtheion caryatids obtained from the British Museum support, at least visually, the large canopy. These controversial features were intended by Lubetkin to be read 'not as part of the building but as a garden ornament'. The main entrance leads to a boomerang-shaped foyer. Ramps on either side lead to two separate lifts, which open directly into the flats.

There are separate lifts and stairs for tradespersons and servants. Lubetkin designed the penthouse as his London home with two bedrooms, two bathrooms, and a large living room under a curved roof. The apartment had a very personal and unorthodox modernist interior with furniture, mostly designed by Lubetkin himself. He only lived there briefly, since at the outbreak of the Second World War he took up farming in Gloucestershire, where he lived until 1969.

3

Highpoint II: The entrance canopy is supported by sculptures of female figures (caryatids), a feature that, at the time of construction, was believed to be a sign that Lubetkin had forsaken the Modern Movement.

Source: Philipp Meuser

Isokon Building
1–32 Lawn Road, Camden
Wells Coates
1934
⊖ Belsize Park

037 B

The Isokon Building – initially known as the Lawn Road Flats – was listed Grade II in 1974 as '1, 1A, 1B, 1C and 1D, and 2–32 Isokon Flats'. The four-storey concrete block was designed in the early 1930s by the expatriate Canadian architect Wells Coates in cooperation with John Craven (Jack) Pritchard (1899–1992) and Rosemary (Molly) Pritchard (1900–1985). Wells Wintemute Coates (1895–1958) spent his youth in Japan. When asked about his aesthetic and functional sensibilities, he referred back to this time. On the advice of his architect mother Sarah Agnes Wintemute Coates, he did not study architecture but engineering. He attended the 1933 Congrès International d'Architecture Moderne (CIAM) and was one of the founders of the MARS group, the British wing of CIAM. The Isokon Building opened on 9 July 1934 and was an experiment in modern urban living. It originally contained 34 units, including two for staff. The ground floor initially comprised four *existenzminimum* flats (dwellings that cater for the minimum level of existence), a two-room flat at one end, a lobby with a porter, two 'minimum flats' as staff quarters, an office, a kitchen, a laundry, a storage room and a large garage. Part of the garage became the porter's lodgings when in 1937 the kitchen and the staff quarters were converted into the Isobar Restaurant, to a design by Marcel Breuer and F. R. S. Yorke. The first, second, and third floors each featured six one-room minimum flats, a large studio-flat at the northern end, and a two-room flat at the southern end. All had space-saving built-in furniture, a bathroom, and a dressing room. Plywood was widely used, both in the apartments and for furniture, as Jack Pritchard was involved with the Estonian

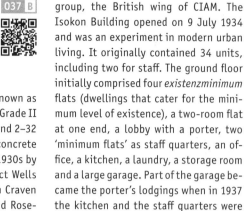

company Venesta (Veneer from Estonia). On the fifth floor there was a 65 m² one-bedroom penthouse. The Pritchards lived there, with their two sons next door in a smaller studio penthouse; they were the only family in the building. Except for the three flats for short-stay tenants, the flats all had tiny kitchens, since there was also a large central kitchen. From there, food could be sent up to the apartments using a dumb waiter. Other services, such as cleaning, laundry, and shoe-shining, were provided within the building. The flats, roof terrace, and most of all the Isobar (a bar, club room, and 20-seat restaurant) became a well-known hotspot for left-leaning artistic and intellectual life in north London. However, the estate also proved to be a perfect refuge for German and Russian spies, including Arnold Deutsch, the agent known for recruiting the Cambridge Five Spy Ring. The writer Agatha Christie wrote her only spy novel, *N or M?* in 1941 while living in Isokon. The penthouses and cantilevered

access balconies are reached via a five-storey stairwell. A sculptural open staircase provides another (discreet) way of entering and leaving the building. The connection between the home and the city is not addressed via the traditional formal street but handled relatively casually through the triangular parking forecourt. This space, shared by cars and pedestrians, emphasises the free-standing position of the building. When Camden Council bought the building in 1972, Ken Livingstone wanted to replace it with a high-rise. Listing prevented this from happening, but poor maintenance and a disastrous allocation policy led to almost irreparable decay. Twenty-five years after first being listed, the building was upgraded to Grade I, the highest category. In 2003, after a competition, the building was completely restored by Avanti Architects, for Notting Hill Housing Association and the Isokon Trust. The Isobar and its adjoining areas could not be revived, and the space was converted into two enlarged *existenzminimum* flats and a one-bedroom flat, accessible from the former tradesperson's entrance. The restoration produced 25 flats for sale under shared ownership for key workers, and another 11 flats (including the penthouse) for the open market. After this restoration, Isokon comprised 36 units (including the penthouses). Avanti also created the Isokon Gallery in the former garage. This exhibition space tells the story of the building, its residents, and the Isokon furniture brand. The name Isokon is short for 'Isometric Unit Construction' and refers to the isometric 3D drawing technique Coates favoured and the 'unit dwellings' they were to sell. The 'K' taken from *Konstruktivizm* gave it a certain Russian touch. For the Pritchards though, the building was always the Lawn Road Flats and Isokon the name of the furniture company. Although Wells Coates's building was never intended as social housing, its innovative architecture of self-chosen *existenzminimum* flats had the appearance of mass-housing and influenced later council housing. Coates never designed social housing; to further realise his architectural ideas, he had to find high-end clients.

037 B

Isokon Building: The parking forecourt, a novelty at the time of construction

10 Palace Gate
10 Palace Gate,
Kensington and Chelsea
Wells Coates
1939
🔵 Gloucester Road

Wells Coates (1895–1958) was not so much an architect but more of a product and interior designer, and above all an inventor. In her books on her father and his work, Laura Cohn describes some of his pioneering architectural designs inventions as equal to a new type of sailing boat or door handle. In 10 Palace Gate, Coates experimented with what he called 'planning in section'. Inspired by his own almost 4-metre-high apartment, where he created a bathroom under a raised bed, he developed, by drawing isometric sections, his '3-2 system'. This meant that three floors in one part of a building are as high as two floors in another part. The system generates living rooms of 'double' height. An advantage of it is that two (or more) flats interlock within the height of three floors. The single-height rooms at the middle (access) level can be combined with either the top or bottom flat or into the adjoining flats, without structural alteration. This flexibility, both vertical and horizontal, in the size of the dwellings, and the complexity of the building process deterred developers. However, late

in 1936 Coates found Randal Bell, a developer who was looking for something other than the conventional flats he had been building up to that point. 10 Palace Gate was constructed in reinforced concrete with an artificial stone cladding and was completed and first occupied in 1939. Potential residents had a wide choice of sizes and furnishings, and the development was a success. In a more elaborate version of the underlying system, two sets of three floors are stacked. The 3-2 system is again expressed in the fenestration: four rows of four high living room windows on the eastern (garden) side are placed next to the rows of windows of single-height rooms. The ordering of the open galleries

Source: Bob Bronshoff (all pictures)

on the façade also shows this system but in a subtler way. To make full use of the plot, a small, slightly concave block of seven storeys, each housing a two-room flat, was erected before the main volume and then connected to it. This hides part of the Grade II* listed building.

3

Sassoon House
St Mary's Road, Southwark
Maxwell Fry, Elizabeth Denby
1934
Queens Road Peckham

039 E

Sassoon House, built in 1934, is the result of a collaboration between the architect Maxwell Fry (1899–1987) and the social reformer Elizabeth Denby (1894–1965). Denby, who had studied sociology, had previously researched social housing around Europe and established herself as a 'housing consultant' – a profession she more or less invented for herself. Although frequently overlooked today, Denby was a prominent social reformer and viewed the solution to the problems of the city dweller as being urban revitalisation rather than garden suburbs. She was associated with the Pioneer Health Centre in Peckham, a community centre that alongside healthcare provided leisure facilities and accommodated a group studying the effect of urban life on city dwellers. It was through this organisation that she met the philanthropist Mozelle Sassoon (1872–1964), who wanted to fund the construction of a block of flats in memory of her late son. In 1933 the organisation donated a plot of land

and Sassoon House was built to complement its activities. The five-storey building originally had a total of 20 flats. Each floor contained two two-bedroom flats in the middle and two three-bedroom at the ends. On the ground floor, one three-bed flat was reduced to a two-bed flat to provide access to the stairwell inside the volume featuring a mural of a horse and rider on the exterior. There were short galleries on the north side. The south side of Sassoon House was symmetrical, with projecting balconies at the ends and recessed balconies in the middle. All balconies had built-in window boxes for plants. The windows were made from steel and painted blue. Every flat had a separate bathroom and kitchen – a novelty for the day as baths were often situated in the kitchen. The kitchens had standard units and a combination heater/cooking stove. With this, Denby and Fry introduced their 'minimum' layout into workers' housing in Britain. The layout kept building costs low and created a labour-saving home environment for families. Unfortunately, the interior layout was completely changed in a modernisation scheme in the 1980s. Sassoon House was listed in 1998. It now forms part of the housing stock of the London Borough of Southwark.

3

Source: Philipp Meuser (all pictures)

Kensal House

1–68 Ladbroke Grove,
Kensington and Chelsea
Maxwell Fry, Elizabeth Denby
1937

040 B

⊖ Kensal Green

Maxwell Fry and Elisabeth Denby's collaboration continued after Sassoon House (039). They worked on Kensal House from 1933 to 1937. This experimental social-housing scheme was commissioned and financed by the Gas, Light and Coke Company. The firm provided the site, and by only fitting gas appliances, aimed to prove that in modern housing gas could be cheaper than electricity. Kensal House is an ensemble of three residential blocks and a semi-circular nursery building. The residential blocks each have communal spaces at ground-floor level, such as social clubs, and the nursery follows the line of the gasometer that once occupied the site. The two larger five-storey blocks are both set at an angle to the road and run approximately north to south. The eastern block of these two is located so that the morning sun can enter the bedrooms on the east side of the flats and the afternoon sun the living rooms. The western block is twice as long as the eastern; its southern part runs parallel to the eastern block while its northern part curves round to align with the main road. The third and shortest block is L-shaped. It is four floors high and the short side of the 'L' is perpendicular to the road. The 68 dwellings over the three blocks initially housed 380 residents, including 244 children. All flats have the same three-bedroom floor

plan except for those at ground-floor level, which have one bedroom less to allow space for the entrance hall and the associated storage. Each flat had two balconies: one adjacent to the living room for relaxation, the other a loggia with perforated concrete balustrade for hanging out washing. The modernist language can be seen as a continuation of Fry's work, but the concepts and some of the design owed much to Denby. After the project was completed, Fry failed to acknowledge Denby's role in both Sassoon and Kensal houses in publications of the day (though he later made attempts to correct this). They did not work together again afterwards: Denby continued her work as a housing expert and in 1938 published *Europe Rehoused*, and Fry continued as an architect, forming a partnership with Jane Drew.

Source: Philipp Meuser (all pictures)

3

Kent House

041 B

13–17 Ferdinand Street, Camden
Connell, Ward & Lucas
1935

🔵 Chalk Farm

Kent House is the only social-housing project by Connell, Ward & Lucas, an office comprising Amyas Connell (1901–1980), Basil Ward (1902–1976), and Colin Lucas (1906–1984). It is also one of the few examples of workers' housing designed by Modern Movement architects in Britain before the Second World War. This relatively small project of 15 flats and a (former fish-and-chip) shop was commissioned by the Northern Group of the St Pancras Home Improvement Society. It consists of two blocks arranged one in front of the other at an oblique angle: one fronts the street, the other faces the courtyard in between (now a playground). Often seen as identical, the blocks are in fact different heights: the front block has five storeys and the rear four. Both have roof terraces and balconies with rounded rails. Both also have one three- and one two-bedroom flat on each floor, all accessible from an asymmetrically placed entrance. The staircase was originally open, and the lift is a later addition. Although the floor plans for each block are basically

the same, the front block has one oblique corner to adapt to the shape of the plot. At ground level, half of the floor plan is occupied by a dwelling and storage space, and the rest is open. The asymmetry in the plan can also be read from the subtle asymmetry of the façades. Historic England listed Kent House Grade II in 1993, because of its pioneering design and the quality of detailing not usually seen in social housing. During recent renovations the single glazing was replaced, the kitchens and bathrooms and other services were upgraded, the exterior repainted, and the balcony balustrades raised.

Source: Philipp Meuser (all pictures)

Lennox House
1–35 Cresset Road, Hackney
John Eric Miers Macgregor
1937
⌨ Homerton

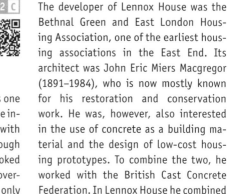

042 C

This five storey-complex of 35 flats is one of the most innovative buildings of the interwar period: it was the first housing with a ziggurat design in London. Although listed Grade II, it is often overlooked in architectural guidebooks and overviews. When it is noted, it is often only seen as a neo-Georgian precursor of later, more monumental modernist developments, such as the Brunswick Centre (063) and the Alexandra Road Estate (072).

The developer of Lennox House was the Bethnal Green and East London Housing Association, one of the earliest housing associations in the East End. Its architect was John Eric Miers Macgregor (1891–1984), who is now mostly known for his restoration and conservation work. He was, however, also interested in the use of concrete as a building material and the design of low-cost housing prototypes. To combine the two, he worked with the British Cast Concrete Federation. In Lennox House he combined an experimental concrete A-frame with more traditional brick infill and cladding. The complex consists of three blocks: two ziggurat-type blocks and one more

conventional block. The ziggurat blocks have three-bedroom flats on the ground floor, one-bedroom flats on the top floor, and two-bedroom flats on the floors in between. Except for the ground-floor apartments, all flats have wide balconies, accessible from the living room. The area between the ziggurat blocks was intended for a market to provide income for residents. However, zoning regulations prohibited this, and the space was instead used for storage, including air-raid equipment and a decontamination centre during the Second World War. The design also included facilities for its residents, such as clothes lines, window boxes, space for prams and safe children's play areas on the balconies. Lennox House was opened by the Duke of Kent in 1937. In the 1940s the Society for Women Housing Managers cited it as an exemplary housing project to be copied. The building was refurbished in the 1980s and again in 2008.

3

White City
Australia Road,
Hammersmith and Fulham
LCC Architects' Department
1939–1953
⊖ White City

043 B

was Pete Townshend (born 1945), the gui-
tarist of the Who. His 1985 solo album
White City: A Novel referred to the place
where he grew up. In his songs, White City
was 'a black, violent place' from his window he saw 'roads leading to darkness,
leading home'.

The original White City (or Great White
City) was an 80-hectare complex of pal-
aces, halls, and Venetian-style canals, as
well as a large stadium. It opened in 1908,
and that year hosted both the first Olympic
Games in England and the Franco-British
Exhibition, a fair celebrating European
colonialism. After the last exhibition in
1914, the complex fell into disrepair and
much of the land was used for housing. In
1935, London County Council (LCC) bought
20 hectares of the site and produced plans
for an estate of 2,286 flats. This was supposed to house some 11,000 people in
49 five-storey tenement blocks. When the
estate was finished in 1953, it contained
2,011 homes in 35 blocks and housed
8,885 people, by and large fulfilling LCC's
ambitions to erect large-scale housing
to rehouse large numbers of people from
slum clearances. The estate exhibits a civ-
il equality – all building blocks look the
same – as well as a non-hierarchical composition – the neighbourhood facilities
are not placed in a central location but in
a long strip through the estate. With this
strip oriented north to south, the buildings gained morning and evening sunshine
on their east- and west-facing façades. All
living space was therefore situated at the
western side and bedrooms on the eastern side. Modern European views regard-
ing mass-housing were the driving force
behind the large-scale buildings. The
LCC wanted to implement the long, thin
row buildings that were being developed
in Germany (*Zeilenbau*) around the same
time. However, this did not work with their
goal to give residents attractive enclosed
green courtyards and houses with access
galleries on both sides of public streets.
They therefore left most of the southern
ends of the courtyards open. The majority
of the estate was finished in the 1950s but
other buildings were added later: Malabar
Court in the 1960s and White City Close in
the 1970s. Over the years, the estate fell
into disrepair. Its most famous resident

Source: Tjerk Ruimschotel (all pictures)

3

Post-war

From 1940 to 1960

Excalibur Estate

1, 3, 5, 7, 25, and 39
Persant Road, Lewisham
Selection Engineering Co.
1946
🚊 Bellingham

044 E

Under the Housing (Temporary Accommodation) Act of 1944, the government provided funds to be spent on erecting dwellings to alleviate the accommodation shortages caused by the Second World War. One of the estates this produced was Excalibur. It comprised 188 prefabricated buildings – 187 bungalows and a church – and was built straight after the war on green open land that originally belonged to the London County Council's Downham Estate. The labourers were Italian and German prisoners of war. The houses arrived as flat-pack kits. Except for the kitchen and bathroom, everything was put together on-site. These Uni-Seco prefab units were manufactured by the Selection Engineering Co., a firm with experience building emergency shelters. They came in two types: Mark II and Mark III. The panels for the units consisted of plywood or timber frames clad in asbestos sheeting and filled with woodwool as insulation. With their modular construction, flat roofs, and distinctive corner windows the homes could be seen as being influenced by the Modern Movement. They proved popular at the time because they had up-to-date amenities such as an indoor toilet, fitted kitchens with fridges, built-in storage, and spacious gardens. Today the Excalibur Estate is one of the few surviving examples of this post-war architecture and town-planning phenomena. In recent years, though, Lewisham Council have demolished most of it to make way for new housing. English Heritage recommended a group of 21 prefabs to be saved, but in the end, only six were listed Grade II: on Persant Road there are four Mark II homes with a side door (1, 3, 5 and 7) and two Mark III homes with a middle door with a small canopy (numbers 25 and 39).

Source: Tjerk Ruimschotel (all pictures)

Churchill Gardens

045 D

Around Churchill Gardens Road,
Westminster
Powell & Moya
1946–1962
⊖ Pimlico

4

Phillip Powell (1921–2003) and Hidalgo 'Jacko' Moya (1920–1994) were still in their last year at the Architectural Association School when they won the Pimlico Housing competition held by Westminster Council in 1945. When the public exhibition of the entries opened in May 1946, Powell was 25 years old, and Moya had just celebrated his 26th birthday. Inspired by modernist housing on the Continent, they employed an informal urban layout for a mixture of tall slab blocks, lower blocks of maisonettes, and terraced houses. It had to be a high-density development to meet the acute housing shortage in London after the Second World War (originally Westminster Council had wanted to re-plan more than twice the eventual competition site extending north of Lupus Street, including the nineteenth-century terraces designed by Thomas Cubitt). When it was completed in the 1960s, Churchill Gardens was made up of 1,661 dwellings on an area of 12.5 hectares. Its 38 'houses' were contained in 40 blocks, erected in four phases. Massing, heights, access, housing types, and design details were modified as building progressed. However, the starting point always remained the same: blocks running along the streets bordering the estate and other main roads, high-rise blocks mostly parallel north–south inside the estate, and lower blocks sprinkled throughout the estate and along the riverside. Phase one (1946–1949) consisted of 11 blocks, four of them nine-storeys high with extruded glazed staircases along the eastern side of the blocks. These four (Chaucer, Coleridge, Shelley, and Keats houses) were listed Grade II in 1998. During this phase, a seven-storey block with maisonettes over shops (De Quincey House) was built parallel to Lupus Street and six four-storey blocks with maisonettes were constructed behind it. The estate's other block with shops (Littleton House) was part of the third phase. In phase two (1949–1952)

the three blocks were built: seven-storey Nash House with flats rather than shops at the ground floor, and Gilbert and Sullivan houses, both ten-storeys high, marking the entrance to the estate. This trio was also listed Grade II in 1998. Phase three (1952–1957) filled the area between the buildings of phases one and two, sometimes carrying on earlier building types. Phase four (1957–1962) reveals the change, in the early 1960s, from a composition of simple freestanding blocks to more complex structures. Instead of four small four-storey blocks and two long high-rise slabs facing Calverton Street, a continuous assembly of seven five-storey blocks meanders parallel to the street. The middle part is set back from the street and bridges Churchill Gardens Road. Throughout the estate existing buildings like churches, pubs, and schools were retained and expanded. The estate was the first in the UK to have a district heating system. The round glazed accumulator tower (listed Grade II) was built to collect the waste heat from Battersea Power Station. Despite the dense tower blocks, the estate has a feeling of openness, generated by its informal layout and green spaces.

Churchill Gardens: The road of the same name with the former
heat accumulator tower for the district heating system, which
used hot water from Battersea Power Station across the Thames

4

Spa Green Estate
Roseberry Avenue, Islington
Tecton/Berthold Lubetkin
1938–1950

🔴 Angel

In 1938, Berthold Lubetkin and his firm Tecton were commissioned by the Borough of Finsbury to design working-class housing on a site opposite Sadler's Wells Theatre. Bomb damage sustained during the Second World War enlarged the site and necessitated changes to the brief. This enabled Lubetkin to craft a three-block composition in a complex urban context. Two parallel eight-storey blocks (with lifts and stairs) form opposite sides of a rectangular courtyard containing parking and a playground. In these blocks, Tunbridge and Wells houses, the bedrooms face the quiet courtyard while the living rooms and balconies overlook the street. The front façade of Tunbridge House aligns with St John Street. Wells House is set at an angle to Rosebery Avenue to provide for a small park opposite Sadler's Wells. The two other sides of the courtyard are defined by a single-storey nursery (built later but planned in the design) and the end façade of the third block, Sadler House. This serpentine block has four storeys, with an extra floor at ground level where the topography of the site allows. Spa Green is the first substantial project in which the engineer Ove Arup's 'egg crate' was employed. This rigid concrete frame connects to the cross-walls and floors, freeing the façade from load-bearing. Lubetkin despised 'elevations by the yard'; here he had the chance to compose his 'chequerboard' or 'tapestry' façades without restriction. The estate was listed Grade II* in 1998.

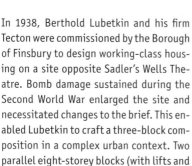

4

Bevin Court

Cruikshank Street, Islington
Skinner, Bailey & Lubetkin
1954
King's Cross St Pancras

047 C

Bevin Court was originally supposed to be named Lenin Court, after the Soviet head of government who had lived on Holford Square in 1902–1903. Berthold Lubetkin had designed a bust of Lenin for the site in 1942. After extensive bomb damage to the square during the Second World War, Finsbury Council purchased the site and commissioned Lubetkin and his firm (the successor to Tecton) with the housing scheme. This estate was the last of three they designed for the council. Unlike in the other two estates (Spa Green and Priory Green [046]), Lubetkin had, for budgetary reasons, to leave out all of the communal facilities. There was to be no community centre, restaurant, or nursery school. Instead, mindful of his well-known dictum 'Nothing is too good for ordinary people!', he focused his energies on creating fitting homes for the working class: an eight-storey Y-shaped block of 118 flats with a spectacular staircase at its heart and a four-storey building of 12 maisonettes (Holford House). The Y-shaped plan of the eight-storey building ensures no northern aspect for the flats. It has a reinforced concrete box frame clad in precast aggregate panels. There are two wings of one- and two-bedroom flats and one of three-bedroom maisonettes. All homes are accessed via spectacular curved balconies. The balconies are reached by various flights of stairs joined via landing platforms. These platforms are arranged at intervals on a column in the middle of the cylindrical space. The Grade II* listing description by Historic England in 1998 lyrically describes this stairwell as 'Lubetkin's most powerful circular ramp since the Penguin Pool (in London Zoo), adapted for humans.' The building was rechristened after the Foreign Secretary Ernest Bevin (1881–1951), a firm anti-communist. Rumour has it that Lubetkin buried the bust of Lenin in the foundations of the building, possibly even under the stairwell.

4

Source: Bob Bronshoff (all pictures)

Bevin Court: Piranesian view of the central stairwell

4

Passfields

Passfields, Lewisham
Fry, Drew & Partners
1950
⌨ Bellingham

048 E

This remarkable group of four housing blocks was intended as a model development equipped with up-to-date facilities. The latter included a lift, a laundry and a workshop, as well as its own playground and gardens. Fry, Drew & Partners, a well-known modernist practice, designed three three storey blocks and a longer L-shaped volume. They arranged the three blocks, each comprising two two-bedroom and ten three-bedroom flats, at right angles to Bromley Road. The longer and taller L-shaped volume (five-storeys high – the maximum height permitted at the time) follows the perimeter of the site opposite the road. By placing all of the blocks within communal gardens and enclosing the site with the L-shaped volume, the architects' intended to generate a sense of community. The long L-shaped volume contains two rows of maisonettes set over 11 one-bedroom flats. The 24 maisonettes are reached via access galleries, which themselves are reached via two staircases that are prominent features of the façade. At ground-floor level, next to the workshop and office, there is a way through to the rear playground and parking. This picturesque ensemble is of particular significance because of its clever incorporation of maisonettes. Passfields was acclaimed at the time and received a Festival of Britain Merit Award in 1951. It was listed Grade II in 1998 and refurbished in the early 2010s.

4

Source: Philipp Meuser

Source: Tjerk Ruimschotel

Lansbury Estate
Area west of Chrisp Street
Market Square, Tower Hamlets
LCC Architects' Department/
Arthur Ling et al.
1951
All Saints

049 C

In 1951, a century after the Great Exhibition, where Prince Albert's Model Cottages were shown (002), the Festival of Britain took place. This nationwide celebration of British arts, industry, and technology included an exhibition of architecture, town planning, and building research. Instead of only constructing a new building to house an exhibition, the authorities chose to display a recently redeveloped area in London, at the suggestion of the architect and planner

Frederick Gibberd. The location selected was the Lansbury Estate, the first section of a new neighbourhood. The site, named after George Lansbury (1859–1940), the former Mayor of Poplar and leader of the Labour Party in the 1930s, was much larger than the main festival exhibition. It was a self-contained part of the postwar metropolis with shops, schools, churches, and houses, and displayed a range of new housing and building types, to be completed for occupation after the festival was over. The 'live exhibition' ran from May to September 1951. Gibberd designed the pedestrianised shopping centre around the Market Square (including the clock tower built in 1952) but was not responsible for the town planning. A master plan showing heights, massing, and open spaces, and probably also

guidelines for using stock-brick walls and slate roofs, was prepared by Arthur Ling (1913–1995) from the Planning Division of the London County Council (LCC). Private architects mainly undertook the design of individual buildings, like housing blocks, homes for the elderly, schools, and churches. However, the Lansbury Estate was too small to show the 'neighbourhood' planning concept that Gibberd also wanted to implement in New Towns. The approach broke a municipality down into several smaller areas with a defined population. Ideally, this would be a community as in the past but minus the overcrowding, inadequate buildings, and health hazards. A fundamental principle was to move 1.5 million people from the metropolis – in particular the East End – to the less-crowded New Towns in

the surrounding countryside, outside the County of London. On one of the exhibition pavilions, visitors could acquaint themselves with this new doctrine, developed by Patrick Abercrombie (1879–1957) and LCC's John Forshaw (1895–1973) during wartime. Today, none of the housing is listed, but the Lansbury Estate was designated a conservation area in 1997.

4

Source: Bob Bronshoff (all pictures)

Loughborough Estate
Around Loughborough Road
and Barrington Road, Lambeth
*LCC Architects' Department/
Gillian Margaret Howell*
1953–1957

050 E

Loughborough Junction

The housing shortage following the Second World War meant that London County Council (LCC) had to become more efficient. To achieve this, they made the Valuer's Department responsible for housing (previously they had only bought and managed sites). The department's preferred solution was to erect large estates with designs dictated by considerations of economy and speed, rather than reflections on housing and architecture. In 1947, when Robert Matthew (1906–1975) was appointed as head of the LCC Architects' Department, he struggled to reverse the decision. He achieved his goal in 1950. This return to the original task came with a renewed enthusiasm for rebuilding bomb-damaged London. In the ensuing period, the department became known as one of the most progressive and radical public architects' departments in the world. The design of the Loughborough Estate was pivotal in regaining the leading position in designing London's housing. Its development took place under various head architects: Matthew led the department until 1953, followed by Leslie Martin (1908–2000) until 1956, and Hubert Bennett (1909–2000) until 1970. A team led by Gillian Margaret Howell (1927–2000) drew up the plan for 1,031 units on the 12.5-hectare site. The main feature is the collection of nine 11-storey-high slab blocks, which include two blocks of maisonettes. The flats at the end of these two blocks overlook the 2.5-hectare area of Wyck Gardens. The majority of the dwellings are contained in the six-storey blocks of flats, the 15 four-storey blocks of maisonettes, the eight terraces of two-storey houses with gardens, and the single three-storey block of flats with six shops on the ground floor. All blocks are constructed from reinforced concrete in a strict geometrical composition. Set in a landscaped setting straddling Loughborough Road and Barrington Road, the housing complex is very much part of

the urban environment, rather than an island like many housing estates. The layout was planned in parallel rows. The taller blocks are oriented on a northwest–southeast axis and the lower ones perpendicular to this, oriented northeast–southwest. Thus, the front door façades and access galleries are situated on the north side of the buildings while the gardens and private

Source: Tjerk Ruimschotel (all pictures)

balconies are on the sunny sides. The maisonette slabs take after Le Corbusier's Unité de Habitation and pre-date the Corbusian slabs of the Alton West Estate in Wandsworth (052). Unlike the blocks in Alton, which had a district heating system, the dwellings at Loughborough had coal heating. Also unlike some blocks in Alton, Loughborough's buildings are not listed.

The Hero of Switzerland pub on the estate is not named after Le Corbusier – an inn of that name has been on the site since 1901. There is a 1960s housing scheme on Loughborough Street in Kennington (Howes & Jackman). Although the two 11-storey slab blocks there are quite similar to those in the Loughborough Estate, they have no relation to the estate in Lambeth.

Alton East
Alton Road, Wandsworth
LCC Architects' Department/
Rosemary Stjernstedt
1951–1955

051 D

🚆 East Putney ⊖ Barnes

In 1951, the London County Council (LCC) Architects' Department made new plans for the land the council had acquired in Roehampton in the late 1940s. During the immediate post-war period another body – the Valuer's Department – had been responsible for housing and wanted to create large-scale housing as quickly and cheaply as possible. Instead of constructing one extensive estate, the Architects' Department decided to divide the site into two (later called Alton East and Alton West [052]). The estate as a whole was supposed to accommodate close to 10,000 people and provide schools, community buildings and shops. Different design strategies were employed in the two parts: one inspired by Swedish urban development and the other by the ideas of Le Corbusier. This caused polarisation in the department. The planning and design of each part was undertaken by different teams of architects, which perhaps demonstrates the liberal attitude of the department's leadership, or its reluctance to choose sides. The first phase of the new housing estate was in Victorian Roehampton Park, which became the Portsmouth Road Estate and later Alton East. It was designed and built between 1951 and 1955 by a team led by Rosemary Stjernstedt (1912–1998), a British architect who had first-hand experience working in Sweden. She had previously worked in the Stockholm and Göteborg planning

Source: Tjerk Ruimschotel (all pictures)

4

departments from 1939 until the end of the Second World War. Stjernstedt had also become the first female architect to achieve Senior Grade I status in a county council. Her team's proposal promoted the idea of a mixed-density development: high-rise blocks of flats and low-rise houses could be planned in such a way that high densities were reached without monotony. Half of the accommodation on the 11.5-hectare site was in high-rise towers and the other was in four-storey maisonettes and two-storey houses. The team adopted Swedish examples and picturesque principles of town planning to arrange point blocks (a name taken from the Swedish term *punkthus*) and meandering blocks of maisonettes on a wooded hillside. The ten point-blocks contained four flats per floor, a space-saving feat achieved by including mechanically ventilated bathrooms, the first in any public housing in Britain. These blocks were clustered near Roehampton Lane and Kingston Road. Here they could stand in the biggest of the former villa gardens on the site, as well as near the top of the hill, enhancing the natural topography. Eight point-blocks were listed in 1983 and the other two were later listed in 1998. The area around Alton East and West was designated a conservation area in 2001.

138

Alton West
Danebury Avenue, Wandsworth
LCC Architects' Department/
Colin Lucas
1954–1959
Barnes

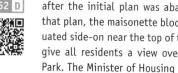

D

Alton West was the second phase of the Alton Estate. The majority of it was constructed from 1954 to 1959. Its designers were a team of architects led by Colin Lucas (1906–1984), an English architect highly influenced by Le Corbusier. Others on the initial team included Bill Howell, John Killick, John Partridge, and Stanley Amis, who later established the practice HKPA. The five much-photographed slab blocks on Highcliffe Drive followed the lead of the Unite d'Habitation in Marseilles. They can be seen as the culmination of London County Council's (LCC) slab-block typology which had been developed at the Loughborough Estate (050) and subsequently at Bentham Road Estate in Hackney (1959). The iconic slabs, however, only emerged

after the initial plan was abandoned. In that plan, the maisonette blocks were situated side-on near the top of the slope to give all residents a view over Richmond Park. The Minister of Housing objected to this 'continuous wall' overlooking a Royal Park, and so in 1953 the orientation of the blocks was changed to its present form: parallel to each other and oblique to the road. This adjustment lent the buildings an even more dramatic look than they would otherwise have had. The dwellings in these 10-storey blocks of maisonettes, raised on pilotis, make up roughly half of the 1,867 homes in Alton West. The estate also includes groups of 12-storey point blocks on lower ground, three- and four-storey terraced houses, bungalows, and a parade of shops. In Alton West, as many of the original trees as possible were preserved. It is a fine example of the superpositioning of a design for social housing on a pre-existing eighteenth-century landscape. The five slab blocks are Grade II* listed, as are the bungalows for the elderly.

Source: Tjerk Ruimschotel (all pictures)

Brandon Estate

Cooks Road, Southwark
LCC Architects' Department/
Ted Hollamby, 1960
◉ Oval

053 E

In the Brandon Estate, new residential buildings are mixed with existing, refurbished ones – an uncommon trait in post-war social-housing developments. When the London County Council (LCC) acquired the site in 1952, the area consisted of streets with ramshackle nineteenth-century terraced housing and derelict bomb sites. Instead of clearing the site entirely as was usual, the LCC choose to renovate the houses on the eastern part and combined this with new buildings constructed according to the plans of Ted Hollamby. Like many architects with left-leaning political views, Edward (Ted)

Hollamby (1921–1999) worked in local authority offices and was well-known for his belief in good design, art for the masses, and social improvement. From 1947 to 1949 his first job as an architect was for the Miners' Welfare Commission. After that, he worked under Leslie Martin as a senior architect at the LCC Architects' Department until 1962. During this period, he was the lead architect for the design of several high-rise housing estates, including the Brandon Estate. The urban layout there comprised traditional streets and squares, cul-de-sacs, new semi-enclosed pedestrian-only landscaped spaces, and a park. More than 180 old houses in Lorrimore Square, Lorrimore Road, and Olney Road were retained and converted into self-contained council-owned flats and maisonettes. A new square, Forsyth Gardens, was created with four-storey

Source: Derk Romschinkl

blocks of maisonettes. The focus of the 15-hectare estate, with its 1,059 new and 328 rehabilitated units, was a pedestrian piazza, Maddock Way. Near its entrance was Napier House, a ten-storey block of flats, flanked by two terraces of shops with maisonettes, a pub, tenants' clubroom, public library, and doctor's surgery. The route east from this piazza led under a seven-storey block of flats and maisonettes into an open, park-like space containing six 18-storey tower blocks – at the time the tallest residential towers in London. Above the ground floor, these point blocks were visually divided into four sets of four storeys. On each floor, there were four two-bedroom flats with a bathroom and separate toilet, an electric drying cupboard, central heating, and constant hot water. Each flat had a full-length private balcony. At the top of the concrete volume of each of the point blocks were four studio penthouses with pitched roofs and private patios. The estate had freestanding sculptures and murals by Henry Moore, Anthony Holloway, and Lynn Easthope, some of which have since been lost. None of the buildings is listed and the estate is not a conservation area. In his final years with the LCC, Hollamby worked on developments in south London and was involved in the first designs for what later became Thamesmead (062). In 1963, he became borough architect for Lambeth, and six years later he became the borough's director of architecture, planning, and development, a position he held until 1981. In these roles, he helped promote innovative low-rise high-density developments, including those at Central Hill (075) and Cressingham Gardens (1967–1979).

4

Golden Lane Estate
Goswell Road/Baltic Street/
Golden Lane/Fann Street,
City of London
Chamberlin, Powell & Bon
1952–1962
⊖ Barbican

054 C

Golden Lane Estate is generally seen as the most successful mixed-use urban development of the 1950s. To build homes for those working in London's financial hub, the Square Mile, the City of London Corporation purchased a heavily bomb-damaged site just inside neighbouring Finsbury in 1951 (the area became part of the City of London in 1994). The City had no plans to establish its own architectural department; instead, they employed private architects, sometimes after a competition like the one for Golden Lane in 1952. Similarly to the Churchill Gardens competition in 1945, this was a big opportunity for architects to acquire a large-scale commission. Some 175 entries were submitted. The winning design was by Geoffry Powell (1920–1999) and marked the start of his partnership with Peter Chamberlin (1919–1978), and Christoph Bon (1921–1999). The three young lecturers, who had all entered their own designs, had decided to work together if one of them won. Although not the winning entry, the plan by Peter and Alison Smithson for 'streets in the sky' managed to gain an almost iconic status, thanks to the couple's promotional skills. They later realised some of these ideas in Robin Hood Gardens in Tower Hamlets (061). The initial brief for Golden Lane was for 300 dwellings, for the most part with one, two, or three bedrooms. However, Powell's initial design altered over time. This was for two main reasons:

4

more land became available near Goswell Road and the council's height constraint of 30 metres was abolished. Realised, in the end, on an area of 3 hectares, the estate today houses about 1,500 people in more than 550 dwellings. The four- and six-storey blocks of maisonettes (Basterfield, Bayer, Cuthbert Harrowing, Stanley Cohen, and Bowater houses) contain two- and three-bedroom dwellings. Seventeen-storey Great Arthur House has 120 flats and then offices on the ground floor, six-storey Cullum Welch House 72 bedsit flats, and seven-storey Hatfield House 14 bedsits and 42 two or three-bedroom maisonettes over a garage. Four-storey Crescent House includes 159 flats, a public house, and 19 shops. Chamberlin, Powell & Bon firmly believed that a housing development should form part of the city and provide facilities for both residents and non-residents. Accordingly, they converted the basements of the site's former buildings into courtyards and carefully landscaped the public areas. Next to the communal gardens there is a tennis court. Two pavilion-like buildings contain collective facilities such as a nursery and an indoor swimming pool. In 1997 the buildings and landscape were listed Grade II. Crescent House, however, was given more importance: it was listed Grade II* because of the way the grid-like composition was adapted to follow the curve of Coswell Road and its clear role as a precursor to the Barbican Estate (066), a more widely known project subsequently designed by the same architects.

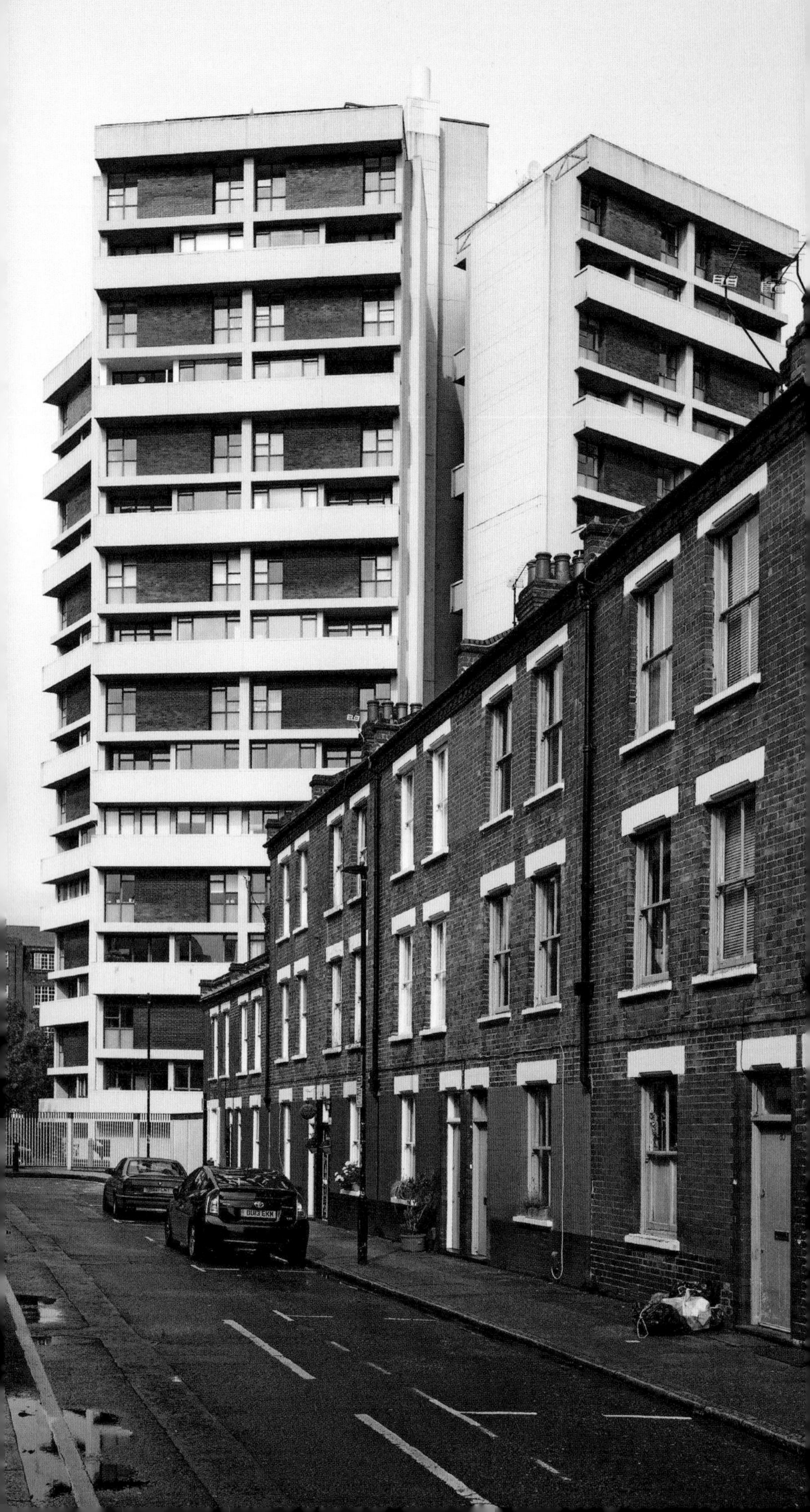

Keeling House
Claredale Street, Tower Hamlets
Denys Lasdun
1955–1959

055 C

🔵 Bethnal Green

4

The idea behind Keeling House goes back 1952, when Denys Lasdun (1914–2001) was commissioned to redevelop a bomb site in Tower Hamlets. There, with his design for Sulkin House, he developed the idea for a 'cluster block': slab blocks set at various angles to a self-contained central tower that holds the lifts and staircase. The blocks only link to the central tower via landings at every other level. In 1955, Lasdun, at the time still a partner at Fry, Drew, Drake & Lasdun, adapted the concept for the large housing development on Claredale Street. This included a low-rise block, Bradley House, which was demolished in 2005, and high-rise Keeling House, which still stands today. Instead of the eight storeys of Sulkin House, Keeling House had sixteen. Like Sulkin House, its plan comprises four towers with different orientations, all linked, at alternate levels, to a freestanding core. The floors with no access landings were designated as activity areas and places to dry laundry. The four towers held 56 two-bedroom maisonettes and 8 bedsits in total. The bedsits were on the fifth floor – visible on the exterior as a deviation in the rhythm of the horizontal bands in the façades. The flats all had their own balcony and the orientation of the towers allowed sunlight to reach every flat at some time during the course of a day. Keeling House was constructed from 1957 and 1959 in reinforced concrete, with some sections cast on-site and others clad in pre-cast panels. Like many post-war modernist housing projects, the building deteriorated in the 1970s and 1980s. In 1992, as the structure became dangerous, and residents had to move out. A year later the Borough of Tower Hamlets decided to demolish the building. There were calls to save it and that year it was listed Grade II* – the first tower block to achieve this status. Due to lack of funds, Tower Hamlets was unable to restore the building, so they sold it to Lincoln Holding, a private developer. Over the next two years, it was refurbished by Munkenbeck & Marshall. The key feature of the renovation was the introduction of a glass foyer for a secure entrance and a concierge. The eight top-floor maisonettes were turned into high-end penthouses, and the boiler room and disused water tank were transformed into two-bedroom maisonettes. Just before his death in 2001, Lasdun visited the project. He was happy about the renovations but regretted that this piece of social housing had to be sold to the private sector to prevent demolition.

Source: Bob Bronshoff (all pictures)

26 St James's Place
26 St James's Place, Westminster
Denys Lasdun & Partners
1959–1960
⊖ Green Park

The destruction of two Georgian houses during the Second World War provided the site for this brutalist block of eight high-end flats. The goal of Denys Lasdun's design was, as stated in *Architectural Design* in 1961, was to produce a building 'which would, in terms of urban renewal, concern itself with the relationship between buildings of historic interest and modern architecture'. He applied this notion with the same zeal as he had done for the social housing in Usk and Claredale streets (Keeling House [055]), completed the previous year. The main volume of 26 St James's Place is constructed from reinforced concrete and clad in horizontal bands of light-grey granite. The roof overhangs are covered with white mosaic tiles. The building contains four four-bedroom flats, two three-bedroom flats, a two-bedroom flat

with garden on the ground floor, and a two-bedroom penthouse with roof garden. All include maid's quarters. Next to the main staircase and lift is a smaller lift and staircase for servants and tradespersons. In the basement there is a garage and a flat for the caretaker. The large apartments on the first and fourth floors have a living room that is one and a half floors high, while at the third and sixth floor the living room is half a storey down and reached by a short flight of stairs. In between, the two apartments on the second and fifth floors have an L-shape layout that wraps around the two high-ceilinged living rooms in the south corner. Their balconies overlook Green Park. The ground-floor two-bedroom flat sits behind the lobby. The penthouse is set back on the seventh floor and covered by a cantilevered roof. Lasdun's split-level plan was likely influenced by his work with Berthold Lubetkin and Wells Coates on the layouts for Highpoint II (036) and 10 Palace Gate (038). The block at 26 St James's Place was Grade II* listed in 1998, five years after Keeling House.

Source: Philipp Meuser (all pictures)

4

Parkleys Estate
Off Upper Ham Road,
Richmond upon Thames
Eric Lyons, Ivor Cunningham
1955
🖵 Norbiton

Architects Eric Lyons (1912–1980) and Geoffrey Townsend (1911–1990) worked together on several post-war private developments. However, in 1953 Townsend decided to become a real-estate developer and so had to give up his membership of the Royal Institute of British Architects (RIBA). Parkleys Estate was their first major work together as Span Developments Ltd, the firm they set up to 'span the gap between the suburban monotony of the typical speculative building and the architecturally designed individually built residence'. The project was initially called Bargood Estates at Ham Common. The estate is built on a triangular site covering an area of 3.3 hectares. Previously there had been a tree nursery on the site. Lyons and Ivor Cunningham (1928–2007), who played a big role in landscaping Lyons' projects, incorporated the existing trees and planting into the scheme. The landscape and series of spaces and views are an integral part of the estate. The layout features one main road, a dead-end street perpendicular to this road, and three interconnected pedestrianised courtyards to the east of the perpendicular road. To the south of the main road and the west of the dead-end street are lines of H-shaped blocks, three storeys high. This strict orthogonal grouping is linked with the surrounding environment by three loosely angled blocks at the western end of the estate fronting Upper Ham Road. There the southern block contains six shops with six maisonettes above. The dwellings are reached by a sculptural staircase, which also leads to the Span Estate Office on the first floor. At the eastern end of the estate, the main road bends and becomes Ham Farm Road. The detached dwellings around Ham Farm Road are part of the development and were individually designed, under the supervision of Span. All buildings are flat-roofed. Their cladding is a mixture of traditional yellow brick, tiles, and coloured surfaces. In total there are 175 flats and 87 garages on the estate. Separate screened off car parks were provided so residents wouldn't have to park alongside the road in front of their homes. To some reviewers, Lyons's squares and terraces were a modernist answer to the Georgian tradition of domestic architecture. The houses were placed in a landscaped suburban setting, but given the high density of dwellings, Span frequently had to convince local planning authorities. Parkleys was developed for first-time buyers, and Span was one of the first companies to promote an interest-only mortgage. Townsend also promoted the concept of a legally constituted residents' association which all buyers were obliged to join. Other conditions of sale were covenants that placed mutual obligations on the residents to contribute to funds for the maintenance of the properties and grounds. All residents are also members of the management company that runs the estate. This early system of management set up by Span has added

Source: Tjerk Ruimschotel (all pictures)

to the excellent condition of the estates today. From the mid-1950s to the end of the 1960s, Span went on to develop more than 70 such schemes, comprising more than 2,100 dwellings, all to the design of Eric Lyons. Of note is the concentration of 20 smaller projects in Blackheath Park in Greenwich (1956–1984) and the few built parts of the master plan for New Ash Green in Kent (1967).

4

The Welfare State

From 1960 to 1980

Cranbrook Estate
Mace Street, Tower Hamlets
Skinner, Bailey & Lubetkin
1965
⬤ Bethnal Green

By the time this project – the last housing scheme by Berthold Lubetkin – was officially opened in 1965, the architect's name had been withdrawn from the firm's title. At that time, Lubetkin was becoming something of a mythical figure, as he was spending an increasing amount of time in the countryside. The project for the Cranbrook Estate had begun in 1957, when Bethnal Green Council declared 7 hectares of Victorian terraces and nearby buildings a 'clearance area' and more than 1,500 residents had to be relocated. Building work on the new estate started quickly. The design was for a mixed neighbourhood, both in terms of housing type and in urban orchestration. It comprised six tower blocks in pairs of decreasing height: two 15-storey blocks, two 13-storey blocks, two 11-storey blocks, and five four-storey

blocks, as well as two- and one-storey houses and a block of shops. In all, there were 529 new dwellings: 43 studio flats, 115 one-bedroom flats, 271 two-bedroom flats, and 100 three-bedroom flats. Inside the estate there is a single main road: Mace Street, the shape of a distorted figure eight, connects to Old Ford Road and Roman Road. The buildings are situated in a free composition along two diagonals. This both links the estate to the surrounding road pattern and follows the directions of the estate boundaries. Through this careful positioning, the high-rise towers seem to twist and turn. When a planned extension of a pedestrian axis from Roman Road Square to Victoria Park did not materialise, Lubetkin created a *trompe-l'oeil* sculpture for the northeast corner of the estate. This is no longer there. Just one part of this remarkable feat of design is listed: the *Blind Beggar and his Dog* statue by Elisabeth Frink (1930–1993), placed in the enclosed communal garden for the elderly residents of the bungalows off Roman Road to enjoy.

Balfron Tower
St Leonard's Road, Tower Hamlets
Ernö Goldfinger
1967

🚇 All Saints

Balfron Tower is the most iconic part of the Brownfield Estate, a scheme designed to rehouse the inhabitants of cleared streets in the area. From the early 1960s onwards, the London County Council (LCC) employed private architectural practices for some of their minor schemes to increase the production of public housing. Ernö Goldfinger, who had previously designed two schools for the LCC, was added to their list of 'approved architects' for housing schemes in 1961. He was to design two estates: Brownfield in Poplar, east London, and Edenham Street (where Trellick Tower was built [060]) in Kensington, west London. Brownfield Estate (initially called Rowlett Street Estate) was constructed in three phases. The first phase, from 1965 to 1967, encompassed the construction of the 27-storey Balfron Tower together with housing for the elderly and shops in St Leonard's Road. Next, 11-storey Carradale House was built in 1967–1968, and finally, 14-storey Glenkerry House and Burcham Street Centre from 1972 onwards. The residential blocks are all laid out according to the same principle: enclosed galleries that serve three floors of flats are connected to a separate tower containing lifts, stairs, and communal facilities. Balfron Tower consists of a covered garage at ground level and 26 residential storeys. The 136 flats and 10 maisonettes are in six different types: A to F. Each gallery served 18 flats, and this communal aspect was included to foster community spirit within the 'streets in the sky'. Type A flats, which have one bedroom, are situated on the gallery floors. Their front doors are next to those of the slightly larger type B units, which have two bedrooms and occupy the floors directly above and below. There are five A and B flats per storey. At the southern end – furthest from the service tower and next to the second staircase – the C and D apartments open to the short side of the building. The flats on the access floor are type C, which has

two bedrooms. The larger three-bedroom flats – type D – are situated on the levels above and below. The type-E maisonettes occupy the first and second floors; their entrances are on the first floor and their bedrooms on the second. The type-F maisonettes have entrances on the sixteenth floor and their bedrooms are on the floor below. Their cantilevered balconies, accessed from the living room, break up the all-encompassing concrete framework. The eastern façade features no private balconies, because of the dual carriageway leading to the Blackwell Tunnel. Balfron Tower and the other buildings on the estate were listed Grade II between 1996 and 2015, and deemed characteristic of the post-war aspirations for good-quality public housing. Over the years the buildings on the estate have changed hands. In 2007, it was sold to a housing association, Poplar HARCA. At that time, it was hoped that tenants could choose to stay while a substantial refurbishment took place. However, by 2014, Poplar HARCA had partnered with the developers London Newcastle, and only Carradale House was to be kept as social housing. Balfron Tower was designated entirely for private sale as a means to ensure funding for the maximum number of

socially rented properties across Poplar HARCA's portfolio. (Glenkerry House has been managed by a cooperative housing association since 1979.) In 2015, Balfron Tower was in a dilapidated state, despite an upgrade to Grade II* listed status. The developers therefore advocated a complete renovation of the original dwellings. New fenestration has changed the external appearance of the building: the windows are a different colour and material to the originals to meet soundproofing and environmental standards. Studio Egret West have overseen the recent update with Ab Rogers Design. The original 1960s design aimed to recreate the street-oriented East End communities in the sky. The service tower not only defined the silhouette of the building, but gave residents shared places for laundry and hobbies, and even included a designated 'jazz/pop' room. When they came to revamp the structure 50 years later, the new architects wanted to modernise the service tower with a communal kitchen and dining room, together with a workshop, cinema, library, gym, and yoga room. The main building was stripped back to its structure, and services and finishes were completely redone. The basic layout remains: long service corridors lead to flats

and maisonettes with open-plan layouts that connect kitchen and living spaces without doors. A total of 140 units have been given this contemporary makeover. Of the original six apartment types, only one of each has been preserved as a 'heritage' apartment to show the architect's original intentions. One of these flats is number 130, a three-bedroom apartment on the top floor, where Ernö Goldfinger and his wife Ursula lived for a couple of months after the opening of the Balfron Tower so they could experience and document the pros and cons of living on a street in the sky.

5

Source: Jarrell Goh, Studio Egret West (all pictures)

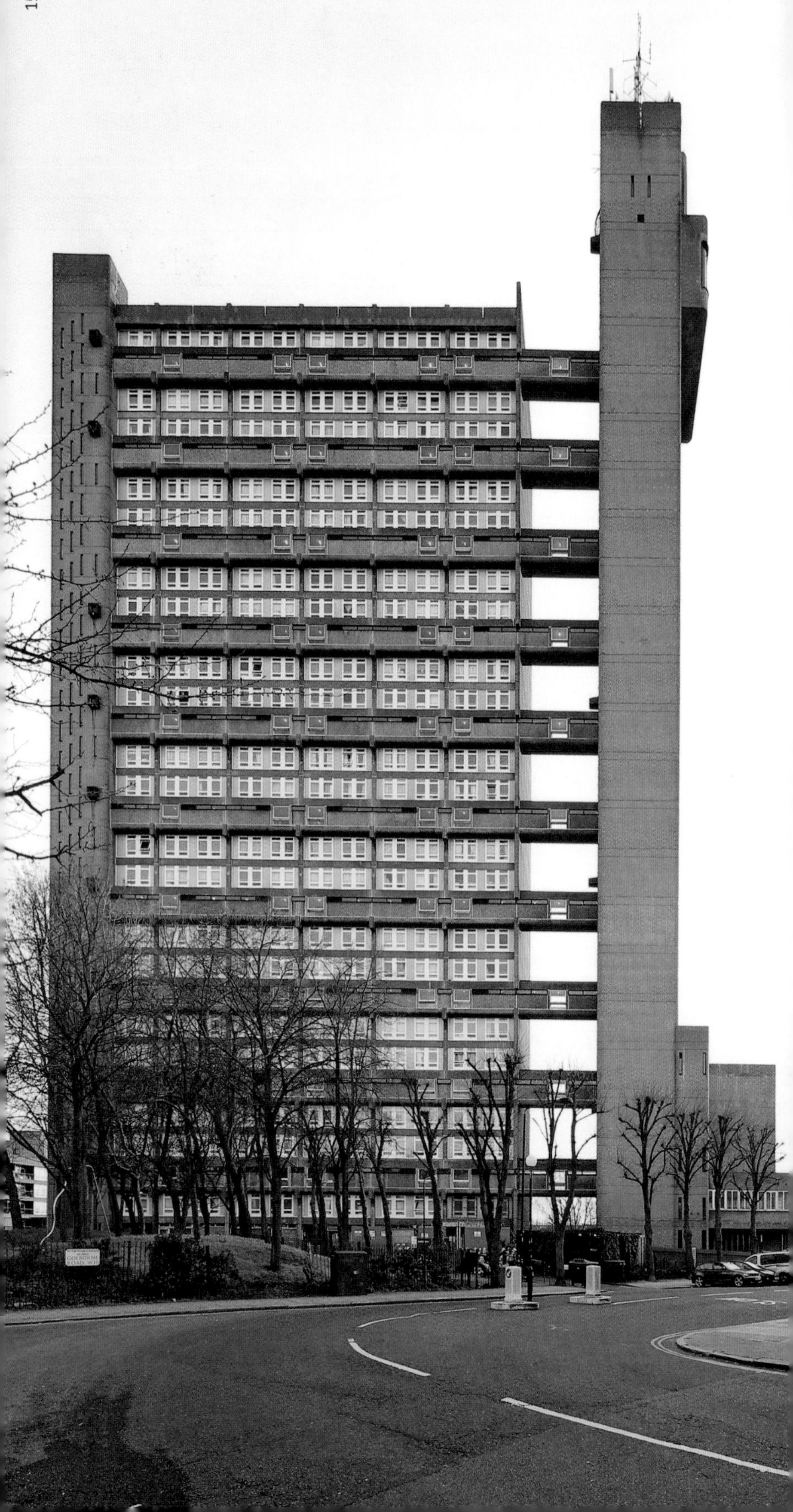
GOLBORNE
ROAD W10

Trellick Tower
Golborne Road,
Kensington and Chelsea
Ernö Goldfinger
1972

🔵 Westbourne Park

060 B

Trellick Tower is the most prominent building on the Cheltenham Estate, a housing scheme situated on a 4.5-hectare site between the Grand Union Canal to the north, the Paddington mainline to the south, and the Great Western Road to the east. In 1963 London County Council (LCC) declared the late-nineteenth-century terraced houses in the area around Edenham Street unfit for habitation. Of the 317 new dwellings on the estate – the Cheltenham Estate as it soon became known – 222 were located in Trellick Tower. The remainder were in five terraces of houses, two six-storey blocks of flats and maisonettes, and an old people's home (now demolished). The tower is not a single block but two blocks linked by a 35-storey service tower. The main building is 31 storeys tall and houses 180 flats, and the lower annexe seven storeys high and contains 42 dwellings. Both are linked to the service tower on every third floor. The service core incorporates lifts, staircases, and rubbish chutes and has a projecting boiler house on its top floors. Each 'corridor floor' contains six one-bedroom flats, with a storey of two-bedroom flats above and below. The 23rd and 24th floors include five two-storey maisonettes and two flats. The building housed a nursery, a community centre, shops, and offices in one of the lower wings. An improved version of Ernö Goldfinger's Balfron Tower (059), Trellick Tower was built from 1968 to 1972. The remainder of the ensemble was constructed from 1969 to 1973. From the opening of the building until his retirement in 1977, Goldfinger had his office in the lower wing at 19 Golborne Road. With its open-access spaces, the tower became a hub for anti-social behaviour and crime in the decade after it was opened. It perhaps served as the inspiration for the novel *High-Rise*, published in 1975 by the science fiction writer J. G. Ballard, an apocalyptic tale about how a community of people living in a tower block behave at a time of crisis. Over the following decades security measures were implemented and a concierge employed (as stipulated in Goldfinger's design) and the tower became a desirable place to live. In 1998, ten years after Goldfinger's death, it was listed Grade II*. Recent plans to restore the building and renovate the surroundings have not yet been realised.

5

Source: Philipp Meuser (all pictures)

Robin Hood Gardens

Robin Hood Lane, off Poplar High Street, Tower Hamlets
Alison and Peter Smithson
1972, demolished 2018/2019
🚇 Blackwall

061 C

The brutal demolition of this iconic ensemble does not make this entry obsolete. It is instead a sad reminder of all the remarkable housing that could not be listed, restored, or revitalised and has now disappeared forever. Designed by renowned architects and spouses Alison and Peter Smithson, Robin Hood Gardens is an instance of a brutalist housing project whose fame has outlived it. The design for the estate was based on the idea for 'streets in the sky', which was submitted in the competition for the Golden Lane Estate in 1952 (054). After waiting over 15 years, the pair finally translated their housing concepts into reality. At that point, they had already built up an influential practice, predominantly through their teaching work and publishing activities. They had also extensively promoted New Brutalism, a style intended to push modernist architectural principles forwards out of a perceived stagnancy. Built for the Greater London Council (GLC), Robin Hood Gardens was the Smithsons' only council estate and constituted the peak of their vision for social housing. It comprised two maisonette slab blocks facing one another, separated by a green oasis (the estate was originally called Robin Hood Lane but its name was changed to emphasise the importance of the open space). The two slightly curved blocks ran north–south; the eastern block was shorter and ten storeys high, the western block longer but only seven storeys high. Over the ground floor, each set of three levels was served by one long open-access gallery, which had no columns to obstruct the view: an interpretation of an East End street. There were 38 ground-floor flats (and a clubroom) for elderly people. From the outset, it was the intention of the architects to provide as much green space as possible for the central 'stress-free zone' in the form of a protected area, shielded from traffic yet open to surveillance from surrounding flats. The waste materials from demolition and excavation were not transported off-site but placed in a central mound (as for the park on Boundary Street Estate [011]). The architects envisaged that perhaps for the first time, people inside the building could look out of their windows at a slope of rising grass: an unusual experience for Londoners. There were 214 flats in all – more than the 136 the GLC had specified. This higher figure was to reduce the necessary number of homes in a (never realised) future development, nearer to East India Dock Road. The apartments themselves ranged in size from two-person flats up to six-person maisonettes and had spacious interiors. In an attempt to bring the celebrated East End street life up to date, the wide galleries provided enough room for residents to sit in front of their doors and socialise and for children to play. The galleries were designed with plenty of thought for daily life, a quality that is hard to find in many inter- and post-war gallery-access estates. However, Robin Hood Gardens provoked mixed feelings and eventually became part of a larger regeneration area. Although the estate was world famous, an extensive high-profile attempt to obtain listed status for it finally failed in 2015. In 2018 the Victoria and Albert Museum acquired a typical three-storey section of the building, preserving it as a fragment of an extinct example of the brutalist movement.

Source: Tjerk Ruimschotel (all pictures)

156

Thamesmead Area One
Tavy Bridge, Bexley
GLC Architects' Department
1967
🚊 Abbey Wood

062 A

Area One was the first phase of the construction of Thamesmead, a New Town-like development built in the 1960s and 1970s on the eastern edge of the Greater London area. The self-contained town, erected on marshland on the eastern edge of the British capital, was planned as an area of mixed housing, from terraces to 12-storey tower blocks, to house some 60,000 people. The Architects' Department of the Greater London Council (GLC) started to design the project in 1965. They intended to provide 'housing of the future' for those relocated from overcrowded dwellings in inner-city London. Lead architect Robert Rigg learned that in Swedish housing estates, lakes and canals helped lower the levels of crime and vandalism. Following this idea and the general principles of New Town planning, he and his team included expansive green spaces and lakes and waterways in the plan. To combat the potential flooding of the lowland, the original design left the ground level of buildings as garage space and positioned living accommodation at first-floor level or above. To reach the front doors, residents had to use elevated walkways. Area One housed more than 5,000 people in 1,490 dwellings on an area of 20 hectares. The urban fabric consists of two zones of repeated configurations of terraced four- to six-person family houses with individual gardens, grouped around small courtyards. Twelve 13-storey point blocks were placed strategically: four located along

the southern shore of Lake Southmere, six along Yarnton Way, and two adjacent to the local shopping centre. Coralline Walk, a linear block three to five storeys high with four- and five-person maisonettes, and almost 1 kilometre long, shelters Area One from the noise of Harrow Manor Way. In the 1970s, public funds for the project were gradually reduced and the project's design was watered down. Transport links in particular suffered: planned road connections to London were poor and there were no DLR or Tube connections. Plans for a central core for Thamesmead were scrapped. The development didn't attract the desired mix of residents. This all led to deterioration and an infamous reputation, not helped by its use in the 1971 Stanley Kubrick film *A Clockwork Orange*. Most recently, though, the housing association Peabody, in partnership with Greenwich and Bexley councils, the Greater London Authority, and Transport for London, has begun to implement a 30-year regeneration plan for Thamesmead. The plan aims to strengthen the direct connection from Abbey Wood Station to Southmere Lake, demolishing the iconic Coralline Walk in the process. As part of the first phase of the works, the developers will construct a new Civic Square together with 525 homes. A new housing typology consisting of buildings arranged around a shared raised garden divides this scheme into several smaller communities. The new civic building housing a library, nursery, and gym and situated centrally at the edge of the Lake, is expected to act as a social hub. Tavy Bridge Centre has now been renamed Southmere Village. Thamesmead is not under conservation and its unique buildings are not listed.

5

Source: Mark Kramer/private

The Brunswick Centre
1 Bernard Street, Camden
Patrick Hodgkinson
1973
🚇 Russell Square

The Brunswick Centre was Grade II listed in 2000, with English Heritage calling it 'the pioneering example of a megastructure in England: of a scheme which combines several functions of equal importance within a single framework ... of low-rise, high-density housing, a field in which Britain was extremely influential on this scale'. But less than ten years earlier, the structure had been refused listed status, as it was not finished as planned by its architect Patrick Hodgkinson (1930–2016). Whether an eight-storey-tall building can be described as 'low-rise' is questionable, but the design did go through many alterations. Hodgkinson worked on the first scheme from 1959 onwards, together with Leslie Martin, a former London County Council (LCC) architect who had worked on the Loughborough Estate (050). This included negotiations with the LCC for outline planning permission for the private development of a superblock with housing above shops, and below ground, a car park and an art-house cinema. An early design shows the housing stepping inwards to the central spine, though this was changed into terraces stepping away from a central public space for shops and a mixture of 16 different apartment types. After that, there followed a period of re-planning for studio and one- and two-bedroom council flats. The result was a complex of 560 flats in two blocks, O'Donnell Court and Foundling Court, completed in 1973. Both blocks have five floors of housing, with the five on the exterior side beginning at ground level and the five on the inner side above the retail spaces. The pedestrian shopping street between the two blocks links Bernard Street to Tavistock Place. All of the flats have a glazed living room that extends on to the balcony and has a sloping roof. The balconies form the blocks' stepped profiles. Hodgkinson originally wanted his idea for a 'London village' constructed in brick, but reinforced concrete was the final choice. After changes in the developer and specifications, which

resulted in Hodgkinson leaving the project, his design was left unfinished and unpainted. But after he retired in the 1990s, he returned to it, working alongside architectural firm Levitt Bernstein as an advisor on the regeneration and upgrading of the scheme – and finally giving it the coat of cream paint that he had always intended. Back in 1966, David Levitt and David Bernstein had been involved in the Brunswick scheme to adapt the speculative apartments in the original design as low-cost housing for the Borough of Camden. In 2002, they were employed to renovate the complex. By then, it had been listed, though ambitious plans for further additions had failed. A mix of imagination and common sense resulted in their new proposal for a supermarket across the north end of the public space, in line with the original aim of having a 'full stop' at

the end of the pedestrian street. The shop fronts were brought forward to the column line, while canopies offered shoppers protection from the weather. Furthermore, the new landscaping of the public realm reduced the width of the plaza by adding walkways and central seating. The renovation was completed in 2006.

5

Lillington Gardens
Between Tachbrook Street
and Vauxhall Bridge Road,
Westminster
Darbourne & Darke
1964–1972
⊖ Pimlico

In the 1960s, while working in Eric Lyons' office, both John Darbourne (1935–1991) and Geoffrey Darke (1929–2011) entered various housing competitions. Darke, for instance, won second prize in the competition to design the Bishopsfield Estate in Harlow. When, in 1961, 26-year-old Darbourne won the competition for the new housing in Lillington Street in Westminster, he invited Darke to form a partnership. The practice took an office in nearby Churchill Gardens (045), a mixed development of dwellings and shops commissioned by the Borough of Westminster. Construction of Lillington Gardens began in 1964. The works were divided into three phases and was completed in 1972. The estate is made up of 14 blocks, mostly between three and eight storeys high. Its 540 homes house around 2,000 people. The buildings of the first two phases are similar, while the third phase is quite different: the façades are plainer and the building heights lower. This is reflected in the listed status of the different phases: one and two are Grade II* while three is Grade II. However, the estate remains cohesive because of the consistent use of reinforced concrete beams and floors, which can be seen on the red brick elevations – a first in large-scale residential buildings. The repetition of architectural detail and staggered volumes also help achieve a unified aesthetic. The first construction phase lasted from 1964 to 1968 and consisted of six blocks at the north-west end of the site. These blocks also housed two pubs: the Lord High Admiral (now Moo Cantina Pimlico) and the Pimlico Tram (now the Cask Pub and Kitchen), a home for the elderly, and a community centre. The first building to be completed, in 1965, was the massive Electricity Board Transformer Station which originally had a football field on top of it (now a playground and garden). The second phase was implemented between 1967 and 1970. Four relatively low blocks were erected between Tachbrook Street and the Grade I listed Church of St James the Less (1859–1961). The buildings from the third construction phase are situated at the southern end of the estate, north of Rampayne Street. These six blocks, built between 1969 and 1974, incorporate more family houses than the earlier phases. The maisonettes at ground-floor level have their own gardens and walkways provide access to the flats on the upper floors. A library was also added at this stage (now empty). The result of the three phases is a large complex of cantilevered council houses, designed to encourage social interaction. An integral part of it is its green space: the sections between the blocks are landscaped and feature a wide variety of tree types, there are plants and shrubs in built planters on the broad access balconies and walkways, and gardens at ground and roof levels. Lillington Gardens was the first low-rise high-density scheme in the country. It broke with the

Source: Tjerk Ruimschotel (all pictures)

tower and slab-block designs which dom- inated during the 1960s building boom. The estate, which has won four architec- tural awards, was designated a conserva- tion area in 1990. Located to the north of Lillington Gardens is Longmoore Gardens, a smaller housing estate designed by Westminster City Council architects and completed in 1980. It was created as a connecting townscape. Longmoore's four blocks employ the same vocabulary: red- brown brick façades with concrete bands. They are not listed but protected in the conservation area surrounding Lillington. Darbourne & Darke went on to win inter- national competitions to build housing, which was unusual for UK firms of the time; they built housing in Germany and Italy.

5

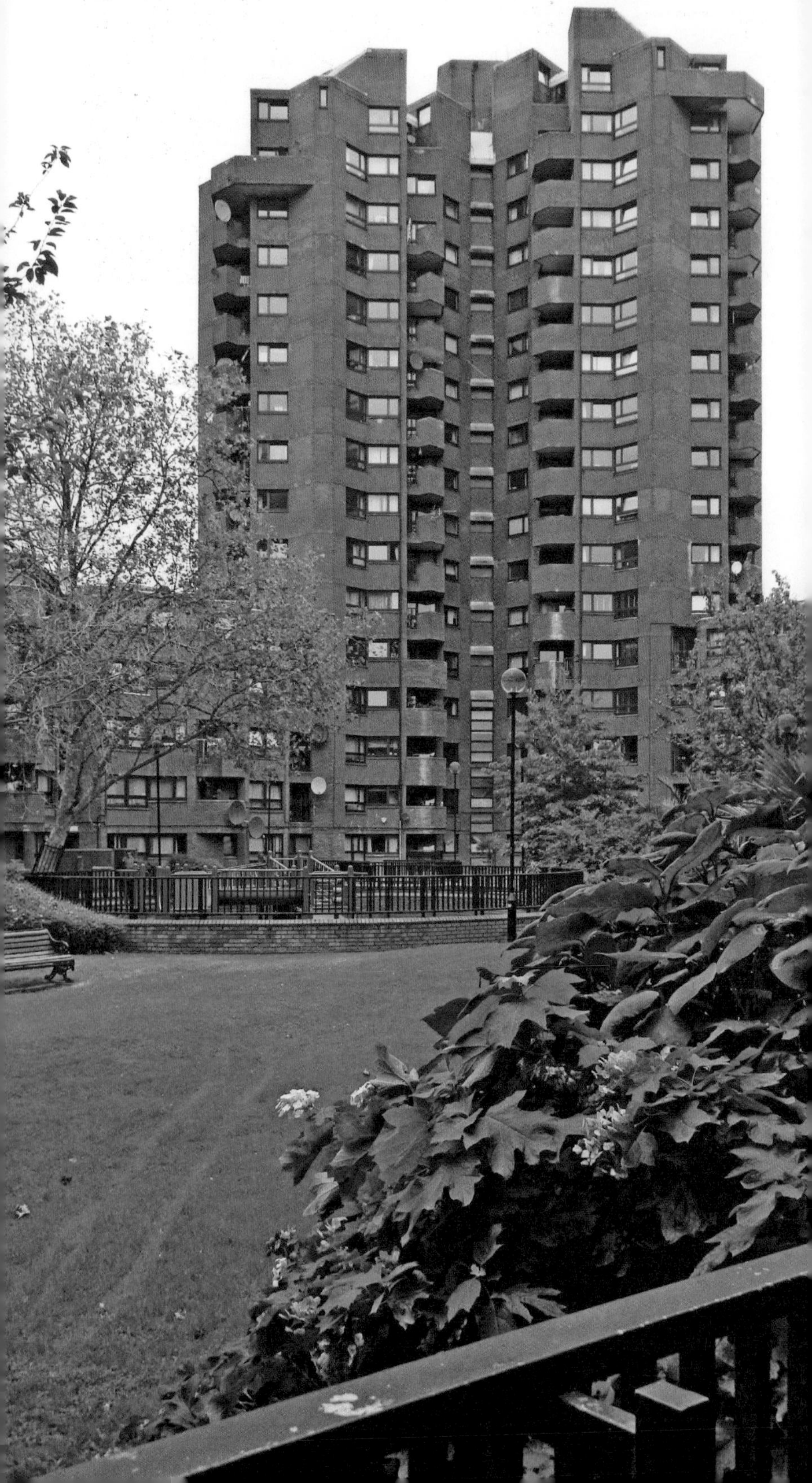

World's End
Blantyre Street,
Kensington and Chelsea
Eric Lyons Cadbury-Brown
Group Partnership
1975–1977
🚇 Fulham Broadway

065 D

The World's End Estate was designed by Eric Lyons for the Metropolitan Borough of Chelsea, a borough where the recent gentrification had left little room for public housing. It is, in fact, one building, since its seven tower blocks are joined with nine six-storey blocks to give an overall shape of a figure of eight. Two walkways, one on the first floor and the other on the fourth floor, connect all the apartments in the lower blocks and the towers. The first-floor walkway is at the same level as two irregularly shaped landscaped courtyards located over the estate's two parking levels. Some parts of this garage were kept free for huge planters to accommodate the root system of the trees that were planted. In 1962 the initial plan set out a housing density that was more than twice as high as the limit set by the London County Council, who duly rejected the proposal. However, the borough council stood their ground, arguing that they had to rehouse all the people from the 4.5 hectares of rundown housing that were to be cleared for the project. It paid off: they won approval for a 742-dwelling estate in December 1966. This might have had something to do with Lyons, who was known for his well-designed private housing estates with Span and had improved on the architectural quality of the original plan. Construction began in December 1969. Due to disruptions such as labour shortages, the project was only completed in April 1977. The first tenants moved in while work was nearing its end, and most properties were occupied between 1975 and 1977. For the project, Lyons worked with Ivor Cunningham, John Metcalfe, and Jim (1913–2009) and Betty Cadbury-Brown (1922–2002), a partnership which lasted from 1967 until 1979. Jim Cadbury-Brown altered Lyons' initial modernist scheme to feature distinctive polygonal shapes. Betty Cadbury-Brown was responsible for the detailing that was needed for the decorative brick cladding on the façades. The seven tower blocks range from 18 to 21 storeys in height. They contain two-bedroom flats, and on the top floor three-bedroom maisonettes. The rest of the dwellings are situated in the linking blocks and are made up of a mixture of studio flats and one- to four-bedroom apartments. The flats are spacious, and when they were built, they provided the relocated residents with amenities they had previously lacked, such as a permanent hot water supply and central heating, modern kitchens, and private balconies. In addition to the courtyards, there is green space next to the River Thames. To the north of the estate are its community facilities, which were erected in the same style. The north side of the estate is home to a few shops and faces the affluent Kings Road, where the average income is six-fold that of the residents of World's End. Although the estate initially came in for criticism for its communal areas, which were open for all and so also to vandalism, today it is seen as a more successful example of high-rise living. It is a distinctive riverside landmark and demonstrates that high-rise and social housing are compatible with high-quality architecture. It is, however, not listed.

5

Source: Tjerk Ruimschotel (all pictures)

World's End: One of the two inner courtyards on a raised level

5

Barbican
Between London Wall and
Silk Street and between
Aldergate Street and Moorgate,
City of London
Chamberlin, Powell & Bon
1969–1976

⊖ Moorgate, Barbican

This vast complex is an example of the generous use of concrete as an eye-catching building material and is therefore often labelled 'brutalist architecture'. However, *béton brut*, from which the term 'brutalism' is derived, is French for 'raw concrete'. The term originally described unfinished concrete, displaying the irregularities (or precision) of the formwork. The Barbican, in contrast, was mostly constructed from concrete poured in-situ and then pick hammered, a costly and labour-intensive process. The brutalist 'as found' use of materials is thus noticeably absent. But since brutalism has become

a household name for sturdy, large-scale buildings with no frills, the estate is regarded as a brutalist icon, albeit for the wrong reason. Beyond the oversized structural elements and all the concrete, it is the design precision that was employed to accommodate an affluent middle-class urban lifestyle that should earn the estate that title. In its architecture, Chamberlin, Powell & Bon accepted and accentuated the realities of mass housing and consumer mass-production. Their first project was the Golden Lane Estate (054), situated immediately north of the Barbican and frequently viewed in terms of being its precursor. Construction of the Barbican itself began in 1963. The opening took place in 1969, and the first tenants moved in then. The other residential buildings were not completed until 1976. Today the complex houses around 4,000 people in 2,014 flats. It covers 40 acres and includes flats with 125 different floor plans. Set up as a 'city within

5

a city', it also contains the Barbican Centre, the City of London School for Girls, the Museum of London, and the Guildhall School of Music and Drama. An artificial ground level links the residential blocks and facilities at a height of 6 metres above ground level. This completely pedestrianised podium was planned in the 1960s as part of a much larger urban network. The housing on the estate primarily consists of six-storey housing blocks of flats (topped by barrel-vaulted penthouses), which enclose rectangular green courtyards. Three 42-storey triangular towers line Beech Street, each with a two- or three-storey penthouse on its stepped top floors. The buildings (including the residential interiors) were listed in 2001. The comprehensive Listed Buildings Management Guidelines were adopted in 2005 and updated in 2012. After Barbican and Golden Lane residents argued for it, a zone including both estates was designated a conservation area.

5

125 Park Road
125 Park Road, Westminster
Farrell & Grimshaw
1970
⊖ St John's Road, Baker Street

067 B

125 Park Road is one of the very few High-Tech residential buildings in London. This approach to visible structural elements, industrial materials, and state of the art technology is more usually applied in commercial buildings. Two of its main proponents were Terry Farrell (born 1938) and Nicholas Grimshaw (born 1939). They met while employed at the London County Council Architects' Department in 1961 and began working together as partners four years later. For the project at 125 Park Road, Farrell drew up the brief and plan. Grimshaw's influence is particularly clear in the corrugated aluminium cladding and rounded corners. The architects were part of a housing cooperative with friends and acquaintances, the Mercury Housing Society, which acted as the client for the building. With finances secured from the Housing Corporation and a building society, the budget was tight. It matched the architects' minimalistic methodology, producing an overall stripped back aesthetic and a repetitive structure. Built in 1970, the 11-floor building originally comprised 41 units: two one-bedroom and two two-bedroom flats on each floor, plus four one-bedroom maisonette penthouses (two of which were inhabited by Farrell and Grimshaw) and a janitor's flat. It has a square plan, with a central reinforced-concrete core housing lifts, stairs, and services and providing structural stability. The structure had no load-bearing elements between core and perimeter. Continuous glazing and well-placed electrical sockets also help provide flexibility inside the dwellings. Partitions could be altered to suit the needs of individual tenants, and some flats have been combined. After half a century, the exterior shows that metal sidings – more normally utilised in factory buildings – can feature in Grade II listed housing. Although 125 Park Road is frequently cited as the first 'core' residential building, Grenfell Tower (Nigel Whitbread/Clifford Wearden Associates), which also had a central service core, was designed and built around the same time.

5

St Bernards

St Bernards, Croydon
Atelier 5
1970
🚉 East Croydon

St Bernards could very well be the only twentieth-century housing project in London (or even Britain) designed by a famous foreign architectural firm. Yet the estate is a conservation area rather than a listed development. The practice responsible for St Bernards was Atelier 5, a Swiss office founded in Basel in 1955 by five young modernist architects. Its first, and later lauded, project was the Siedlung Halen near Berne, a high-density estate of 80 terraced houses stepping down an Alpine slope (1961). In 1966, the private developer Wates Company commissioned the practice to design a similar scheme in Croydon. They asked Atelier 5 to visit the area and to help choose an appropriate site. An area of Park Hill fitted the bill: its landscape and south-facing slope were similar to the estate in Halen. Wates originally planned to construct 161 houses over an area of around 4 hectares, but in the end, they erected just 21 homes. As in Berne, St Bernards consists of staggered rows of houses, but with an overall layout that is triangular in shape. There are three rows of four-bedroom houses (one consisting of three homes, one of four and one of eight) and one row of three-bedroom houses (located over an underground communal garage along Chichester Road). The sloped ground allowed for an unusual two-level layout within the homes, with the bedrooms and bathroom on the lower

Source: Tjerk Ruimschotel (all pictures)

floor, as well as two gardens for each. The main access is through the front gardens on the upper level, which are enclosed by walls. The back gardens are accessed from the lower level, and most have gates to access communal areas beyond. Although pedestrian paths and open spaces link the homes, the enclosed gardens provide privacy for residents and the development appears as one consistent unit.

5

Pollards Hill
Recreation Way, Merton
Richard MacCormac
1971
🚇 Norbury

069 A

This estate in southwest London was commissioned by Merton Architects' Department's lead architect Philip Whittle. Inspired by theoretical studies on perimeter housing, a team led by Richard MacCormac laid out this high-density low-rise scheme in one long ribbon. The string of 562 houses and 288 flats wraps around a public park and rises no higher than three storeys. Based on a Greek key pattern, it generates enclosed outdoor spaces, used to accommodate parking on one side of the 'ribbon' and private gardens on the other. The development originally included a library and a community centre. Both still exist but the library was given a new exterior in the late 2000s. The restrained, perhaps even rigid, aesthetic of the façades and the stark contrast of the urban street with the Arcadian garden side were intended to provide an up-to-date, pleasant environment for council tenants. Despite receiving a RIBA award in 1972, Pollards Hill is not listed. After years of neglect, a major refurbishment scheme is now being carried out.

Dawson's Heights

070 E

Overhill Road, Southwark
*Southwark Architects' Department/
Kate Macintosh*
1972
Forest Hill

Although this estate is officially named Dawson Heights, it is always referred to as Dawson's Heights. Hardly mentioned in regular architectural guides, it is, however, one of the most publicised 'forgotten' housing projects in the British capital. Its architect, Kate Macintosh (born 1937), was just 26 years old when she began work on the design, after winning an in-house competition at Southwark Architects' Department. Her 'Italian hilltop town' in south London consists of two blocks that partially enclose a central courtyard. The blocks, containing 296 flats in total, are a pair of interlocking ziggurats. The blocks vary in height from 3 to 12 storeys, allowing sunlight to reach all of the flats at some point over the day. Originally, there were walkways linking the two blocks, but these were demolished in the 1980s in an attempt to design out crime. All of the flats have private balconies. In the 1960s, the Minister for Housing deemed this an unnecessary luxury for social housing, but Macintosh succeeded in including them at Dawson's Heights as they also serve as necessary fire escapes. The blocks themselves are made up of units of three bays wide: two broad ones and a smaller one in-between. This accommodates a mixture of different dwelling types in ingenious split-level arrangements of floor plans. The taller blocks have a loggia access gallery serving three floors. The height of the blocks is beneficial in terms of density and capturing spectacular views, but also because it provides a small footprint – an advantage because the ground conditions required deep foundations. The two blocks have the same orientation in order to make the most of the light. Their highest portions are offset so that they don't get in the way of the residents' views. The staggering of these simple units, both vertically and horizontal, coupled with the varied streets and staircases in the sky leads to a dazzling image. Unfortunately, the building is not listed.

5

Dawson's Heights: This exemplary council housing is a large, high-density block, yet its varied, brick-clad façades prevent it from being intimidating

Source: Tjerk Ruimschotel

Winscombe Street

22–32 Winscombe Street, Camden

Neave Brown

1965

⊖ Archway

US-born British architect Neave Brown (1929–2018) studied at the Architectural Association in London in the early 1950s. He designed this terrace of five three-storey houses for his own family (no. 30) and a few of his friends, including artist's studio in the scheme (no. 22). Brown saw it as a building for a community or an extended family, rather than as separate homes for five family units. The project, designed in 1963, was feasible because the group of five friends (including Brown) established a housing association, Pentad. With a hundred per cent loan from the Borough of Camden, they managed to acquire the site and start construction. As time went on, members left and joined the group. One of the founding members was Tony Hunt, who was the project engineer and went on to be a key figure in the High-Tech movement in the UK. By the time the work was completed in 1965, Hunt and another person had left Pentad and been replaced by architects Edward Jones and Michael and Patty Hopkins. At the start of the project, Brown obtained a brief from each family independently. He designed the same layout for the five houses, and it met all of their requirements. A main feature of the homes was the section on the lower ground floor (at the time designated for the children), accessed from the street at

the front and opening directly onto the garden at the rear. On the front façade, an enclosed set of steps led up to the front door at upper ground level, where there was a bathroom, open kitchen, and dining area, as well as a terrace with spiral stairs down to the garden. By placing the living room and master bedroom with large pivot door at the top of the houses, Brown maximised the amount of incoming light and views over the communal garden. After living in Winscombe Street for more than 40 years, he and his wife Janet Richardson moved into Dunboyne Road Estate in Gospel Oak. Dunboyne Road was his first housing project for the Borough of Camden, where he worked at the Architects' Department, starting under Sydney Cook (1910–1979) in 1966. In retrospect, Winscombe Street was a forerunner to the legendary public housing schemes that Brown and others produced for Camden Council in the latter part of the 1960s.

5

Source: Philipp Meuser (all pictures)

Alexandra Road Estate

072 B

Rowley Way (formerly
Alexandra Road), Camden
Camden Architects' Department/
Neave Brown
1978

🚇 Swiss Cottage

This estate consists of 518 dwellings in three parallel blocks which run from east to west and curve slightly to follow the railway tracks to the north of them. The seven-storey block adjacent to the railway line is built higher at the back so it acts as a noise barrier. At the front, facing into the estate, the façade is stepped so that the flat roofs can accommodate private outdoor areas on each level. Some of the estate's car parking is located underneath this block. Rowley Way (previously called Alexandra Road), a broad, paved walkway, runs along the front of the block. Access to the ground-floor maisonettes is via this pedestrian street. Between pairs of flats, partially covered staircases lead up to the high-level walkway on the sixth floor and give access to the intermediate flats and the top row of maisonettes. Across from the seven-storey block, on the other side of Rowley Way, is the first of the two four-storey blocks. On the stepped façade of this lower block, open staircases lead to the upper and lower maisonettes. The gardens for these dwellings overlook a public park on the other side of the block. The second four-storey block is located across the park, on Ainsworth Way. At the eastern end of the estate, a complex ensemble of buildings and open spaces accommodate a school, a community centre, the boiler house, shops, and a pub, as well as ramped access to the several pedestrian and vehicle levels. The innovative low-rise high-density scheme was designed by Neave Brown in 1968 for Camden Architects' Department. Building works began in 1972, finally finishing in 1979 after numerous construction difficulties. Following much criticism of the estate and various political power struggles, Brown left the department. He was initially blamed for exceeding deadlines and cost overruns, and though he was exonerated, his

reputation was severely damaged. He did not build in the UK again. Celebrated abroad, he was invited to design housing projects in the Netherlands. All of Brown's three works in Britain have been listed – although with a significant delay between completion and obtaining this status. In August 1993 Alexandra Road became the first (and youngest) post-war housing estate to receive protection under Grade II* listing, after a group of residents, worried about the council's lack of proper maintenance and repair, made an application. Dunboyne Road Estate (1977) was listed in 2010, and Winscombe Street in 2015. Proper acknowledgement came at the very last: in October 2017 he received the Royal Gold Medal of the Royal Institute of British Architects (RIBA). He died in January 2018, enjoying the respect of new generations of housing architects. In recognition of his outstanding work, RIBA launched the Neave Brown Award for Housing in 2019.

5

Loudon Road
49–59 and 61–83 Loudoun Road,
(2-62 Alexandra Place and
1-8 Langtry Walk), Camden
Tom Kay
1980

073 B

🚆 South Hampstead ⬤ Swiss Cottage

These two distinctive buildings facing Loudon Road form part of a later phase of the Alexandra Road redevelopment project. They are located just east of the Alexandra Road Estate (072) and are also listed (Grade II). Like Alexandra Road, the development is low-rise and high-density, but its expression is different: bricks of varying shades of brown, elaborate detailing, and originally, red-painted handrails and window frames. Also in contrast to Alexandra Road, it is mixed-use and consists of workshops and shops as well as housing. At the time Camden Council deemed the area eligible for renewal, the architect who went on to design the project was living on the site. Tom Kay (1935–2007) was born in Haifa (then British Palestine) and grew up in London and Montreal. There his family name, Knopfelmacher, was shortened to Kay. After studying architecture, he worked for Ernö Goldfinger and the London County Council Architects' Department for a short time. Later, after working in Israel, he established his own practice in London in 1964. Together with his wife Adah Nathani, Kay was involved in the politics of public housing and played a part in forming a residents' action group in Camden. The site of the building at 61–83 Loudon Road originally housed several workshops and garages. Kay represented the tenants of these premises, helping push the council to find them new workspaces. When the Borough of Camden commissioned Kay to design the redevelopment of the site at 49–59 Loudon Road, he moved from being an activist to a planning consultant for the project and then finally its architect. The building at 61–83 was subsequently added to his remit a year later. To enhance the entrance to the Alexandra Road Estate, a parade of shops was built along Langtry Walk (numbers 1–8). The building at 61–83 has six shops on the ground floor and two three-bedroom flats on the first floor. The second floor is given over to 12 craft workshops and studio spaces and has a characteristic overhanging profile. The building at 49–59 is square in plan. Its workshop spaces are situated on the ground floor with dwellings above and behind them. An internal access road runs between three two-storey workshops and three small, lower workshops. The flats over the workshops facing 49–59 Loudon Road are reached from (and have addresses at) Alexandra Place. From Alexandra Place, two straight staircases lead to small access courts on the first floor and then continue up to a large communal deck on the second floor.

Source: Tjerk Ruimschotel (all pictures)

5

Branch Hill
074 B

1–42 Spedan Close, Camden
Camden Architects' Department/
Benson & Forsyth
1978
Hampstead

Gordon Benson and Alan Forsyth (both born in 1944) met and worked together in 1966 as students at the Architectural Association. Both joined Camden Architects' Department and assisted on Neave Browne's scheme for Alexandra Road (072). In 1971 Sydney Cook, Camden's chief architect, appointed them as project architects for Branch Hill, a site for which several plans had already been made, but to no avail. Branch Hill was their first project as lead architects (more would follow later at Mansfield Road and Maiden Lane). It consists of 42 semi-detached split-level houses stepping down the hill in rows. Car parking is in an open-fronted garage tucked into the slope above the houses. A main walkway divides the estate into two main sections. The top row of houses has four pairs of homes on one side of the main walkway through the estate. The next two rows have four pairs on the one side and three on the other side. The bottom row has only three pairs parallel to the other sets of three. Because of the intricate close-knit composition and interlocking square elevations and roofscapes, the houses are semi-detached in name only (a requirement stipulated by the council). In fact, they are virtually all part of one built-up area, punctuated by a grid of walkways. The north–south alleys are two metres in width and include steps down the hill. They lead to the front doors, which are situated on the intermediate level of each house. The east–west horizontal walkways provide access to the secondary entrance of each house through the lower garden court. The houses in the top row all have four bedrooms: two at the basement level, and a master bedroom and a smaller one on the cantilevered third level. In the other rows the houses all have three bedrooms. The terraces for the houses in the two upper rows are located on the roofs of the homes in front of them. The houses in the bottom row have no terraces but share courtyard gardens. Spiral stairs link the gardens to the living rooms of these homes. The houses are white-painted concrete while the walkways are red brick. When finished in 1978, the Branch Hill dwellings were called the most expensive council houses in the world. The price of 72,000 pounds sterling each included the cost of the site and the extra works necessitated by the difficult ground conditions. On top of that, the cost of materials and labour increased rapidly in the 1970s. Currently, they are estimated to be worth around 1.4 million pounds on average and are no longer social housing. They were listed Grade II in 2010.

5

Source: Tjerk Ruimschotel (all pictures)

Central Hill

Hawke Road, Lambeth
*Lambeth Architects' Department/
Rosemary Stjernstedt*
1970–1974
🚆 Gipsy Hill

075 E

The Central Hill Estate is one of the most prominent high-density low-rise social housing projects from the post-war period. It was built between 1970 and 1974 by Lambeth Architects' Department, then led by Ted Hollamby. Hollamby brought in Rosemary Stjernstedt from London County Council to lead the team for Central Hill. The estate settles into the hill, taking full advantage of the sloping site and views. The site, which provides panoramic views to the north, towards the City of London, was formerly occupied by large Victorian houses with gardens. Stjernstedt and her team incorporated the existing trees into the layout and kept the buildings within the tree line. The estate itself comprises 374 dwellings, including 212 three- to six-person houses and 162 one- and two-person flats, to suit different age groups and family sizes. The larger homes are in the form of overlapping and interlocking two-storey dwellings in three- and four-storey blocks. The houses are sited along brick pedestrian walkways, with units stepping down one below the other. The ingenious cross-section is reflected in the concrete bands in the brickwork of the end façades. Because of the steep slope,

the houses do not have gardens, but do feature at least one private patio or balcony. Two-person dwellings are situated in the three-storey staircase-access flats at the top of the slope and located over car parking spaces. Living rooms there are on alternate sides of the blocks. One-person flats are on two floors over shops. Communal green and paved landscapes and some community buildings were integrated into the estate. In 2014 Lambeth Council made the decision to redevelop the site, which will mean a complete demolition of the estate. Like other Lambeth estates whose residents are fighting against plans for 'regeneration', such as Cressingham Gardens (Ted Hollamby, Roger Westerman, 1967–1979), Central Hill is not listed.

Source: Tjerk Ruimschotel (all pictures)

Historic England decided against assigning it listed status in 2016. To date, despite residents' protests and proposals to provide for more dwellings and less environmental damage, the council's plans have not altered.

5

Odhams Walk
Odhams Walk. Westminster
Greater London Council/
Donald Ball
1981
🚇 Covent Garden

In the late 1960s, the successor to the London County Council, the Greater London Council (GLC) proposed the comprehensive redevelopment of the area around Covent Garden Market. The plan was widely opposed, since it involved extensive demolition and the relocation of almost all local businesses and residents. Opposition came from local residents in the form of the Covent Garden Community Association, who put pressure on the GLC and ended up implementing their chosen plan. The final version aimed to protect the existing urban fabric, increase the number of houses for local families, and to use the site of the former print works of Odham Press. The estate was designed by a team of GLC architects led by Donald Ball (1938–1992), who had previously worked for Denys Lasdun & Partners. The stout perimeter architecture comes close to the vernacular examples of stacked dwellings favoured by structuralist architects in

the 1970s. It is a successful one-off attempt to design a form of collective urban housing, one based on dwellings that are linked to one another and the city through the interplay of public, private, and semi-public outdoor spaces. Ball's design is a mixed-use complex of 102 houses, located above local amenities, commercial premises, and car parking. The visually appealing, but somewhat difficult to decipher composition of stacked houses is based on two main buildings, formed by dwellings of different sizes: small rectangular two-person flats and larger L-shaped four-to-six-person flats with their own gardens. The stepped elevation inside the block is accomplished by a gradual decrease in the number and size of dwellings per level. Inside the estate, there is a raised public square, connected to the surrounding streets by two pedestrian ramps. There are eight points of entry into the citadel-like complex, including lifts at diagonally opposite corners which lead up to a continuous walkway at third-floor level. This walkway with platforms provides access to the small flats on the third and fourth floors. More than 30 staircases, small access galleries, and large platforms (public, private

5

Source: Philipp Meuser

and in-between) lead to 60 houses, half of them for bigger households. Although the area has become a major tourist attraction, Odhams Walk has remained an oasis in Covent Garden. But the burden of living in an attractive, permeable block turned out to be too high: today only one entrance remains open.

Source: Tjerk Ruimschotel

Crown Reach
145 Grosvenor Road,
Westminster
Nicholas Lacey, 1984
⊖ Pimlico

077 D

Crown Reach is another rare British specimen of stacked dwellings echoing the vernacular examples in the seminal 1964 book *Architecture without Architects* written by Bernard Rudofsky (1905–1988). Its solid, stepped design brought the architect Nicholas Lacey (born 1943) fame: it was selected from more than 400 entries

in a 1977 architectural competition for a prestigious development next to the River Thames. The clients were the Crown Estate Commissioners, who exercise control over the Crown Estate (lands and holdings that belong to the British monarch, but which are run as a commercial business). The project was carried out with the assistance of Robert Maguire and Keith Murray's practice. Aside from the stepped design, another distinctive feature of Lacey's building is its plan: two crescent forms linked by a central entrance hall, one significantly larger

than the other. The shape provides sheltered green space at the riverside, separated from the public Thames footpath. The river-facing side of the building features a staggered play of volumes, clad in enamelled steel panels and glazed tiles. In contrast, the side of the building facing the busy Grosvenor Road has a simple, curved elevation and an almost industrial roof. The crescents' differing heights add drama: the larger one rises from three storeys in the dip in the middle to eight storeys at the two ends, providing spectacular views over the river. The complex contains 60 homes, almost all of which have a unique layout, as well as underground parking. The dwellings each have their own large terrace. These either cantilever out of the building or sit on top of the apartment below. There are a number of offices, light industry, and other buildings at the northern end that help the project blend into its surroundings. The small strip at the southern end accommodates three spacious three-storey town houses and a sculptural smaller end house. The estate was completed in 1983 and is not listed.

Postmodern Era

From 1981 to 2000

St Mark's Road
105–123 St Mark's Road,
1–3 Cowper Terrace,
and St Quintin Avenue,
Kensington and Chelsea
Jeremy and Fenella Dixon
1979
⊖ Ladbroke Grove

078 B

This influential social-housing project celebrates the positive social aspects of urban streets. It featured in The Presence of the Past, the first Venice Architecture Biennale in 1980, where a street created by various architects introduced a global audience to postmodernist buildings. Jeremy Dixon (born 1939) and Fenella Clemens (born 1938) met at the Architectural Association and married and became professional partners until 1989. (After that Dixon formed a partnership with Edward Jones). For them, the project at St Mark's Road began with the idea that London is a city of streets of houses, like the Victorian terraces that surround the site. They wanted to include both historical and recent references in the eclectic design, a typical feature of postmodern buildings. Although the development looks like a collection of 12 houses – 9 in St Mark's Road and 3 around the corner – its appearance is deceptive: each 'house' in fact consists of two narrow houses situated over a small basement flat. At the intersection between the two terraces is a small three-storey block of four flats, each with a large bay window. The houses rise three-storeys above the basement flats,

except for the central units on St Marks Road which have two storeys above the basement flats. The houses have another room in the basement at garden level, as the flats only occupy the front half of the surface. Straight flights of steps lead from the pavement up to the houses and down to the basement flats. The red-brick façades run parallel to the street for the most part, but feature projecting volumes (containing the entrance halls and accommodating a bay window) and almost playful detailing to create a rhythmic look. Behind the façades, the floor plan is angled by 45 degrees to allow space for the houses to turn the street corner and to maintain privacy between neighbouring dwellings. The long, narrow gardens follow the same angle. A maximum contrast in scale

Source: Philipp Meuser

is reached between the public double-fronted street façades and the individual saw-tooth forms of the rear elevations. The scheme was listed Grade II in 2018.

6

Source: Tjerk Ruimschotel

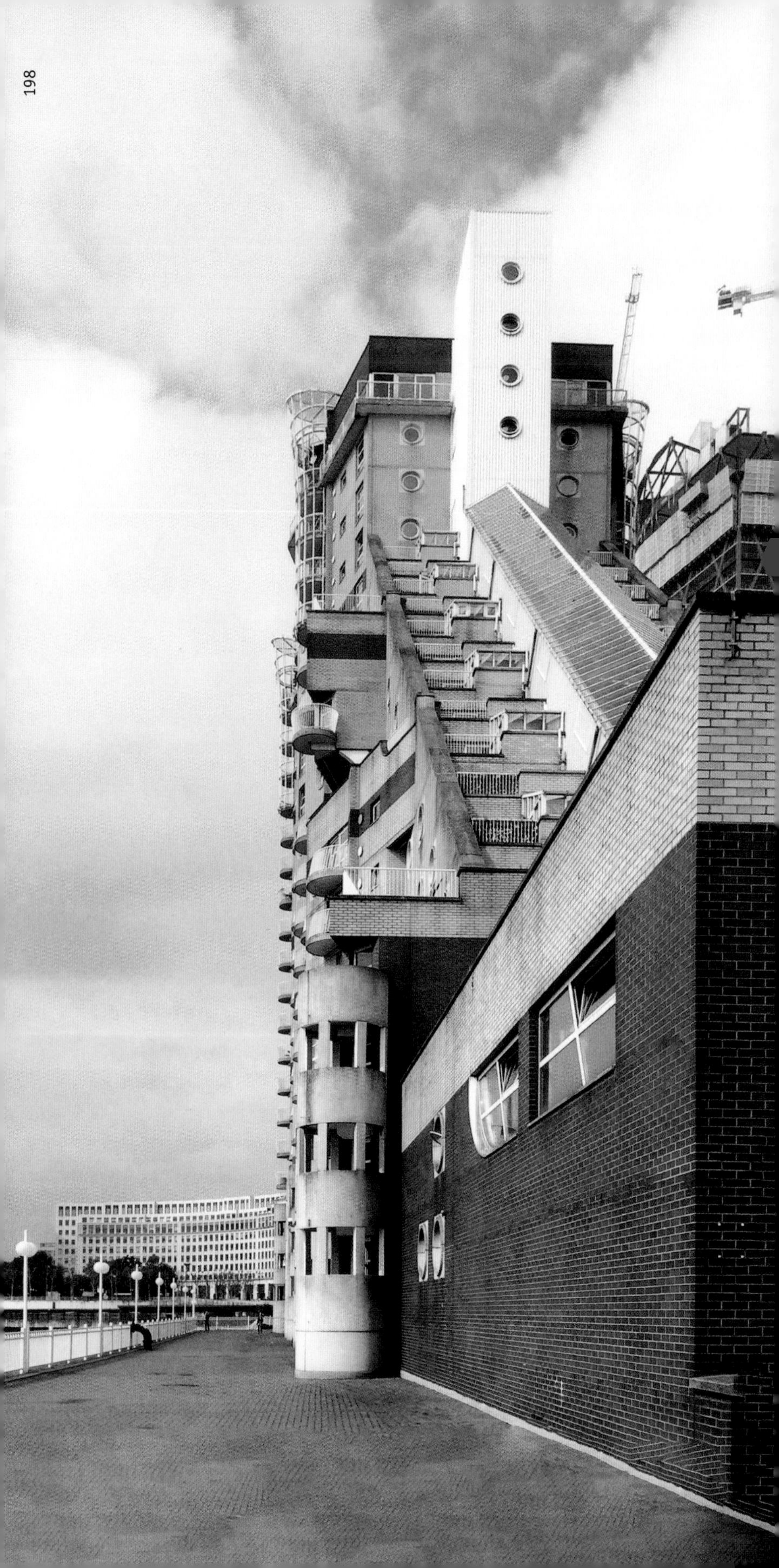

Cascades
2–4 Westferry Road,
Tower Hamlets
CZWG
1988
🖵 ⊖ Canary Wharf

Completed in the late 1980s, Cascades is a prime example of a postmodern residential development of the decade: it references the history and context of its site in an eclectic manner. It was built by CZWG, a practice founded in 1975 by Nick Campbell, Roger Zogolovitch, Rex Wilkinson, and Piers Gough, who met while studying at the Architectural Association. The developer Kentish Homes bought the site with planning permission for three-storey houses in 1985. CZWG, who had previously completed several low-rise projects for the firm, suggested that their design for a 20-storey block could complement the high-rises planned for neighbouring Canary Wharf. The design was accepted by both the client and the London Docklands Development Company, a quango established in 1981 to manage the area and its regeneration. Cascades is located between Westferry Road and the Thames Path. The tower is one of the most spectacular buildings in Docklands: at first sight it has an incomprehensible appearance, the result of the juxtaposition of several detached but interacting elements. The first four storeys of the building, executed in brown brick, are its widest part, while the top four storeys are its narrowest. Over the

twelve storeys in between, the southern end gradually reduces in size behind two walls. The effect is made all the more dramatic by the glazed fire escape, which extends down the sloping side of the building and ends at the volume housing the indoor swimming pool. The alternately positioned conservatories and terraces of the south-facing flats on the slope add yet more interest, as well as a somewhat nautical touch when combined with the building's porthole windows and crow's-nest-like forms. The bulk of the tower consists of two-bedroom apartments, situated behind the accordion-shaped exterior wall. Some interior walls are set perpendicular to these folds, which results in unusual floor plans inside. Every four storeys the reduction in the number of 'normal apartments' is marked by a band of brown bricks in the yellow-brick elevation. Although the building appears to have load-bearing walls (including buttresses), the construction is a concrete frame, which allowed the architects to mould, seemingly at random, the exterior walls with balconies and alcoves. A lower warehouse-like complex, with shops and apartments above, is set at a right angle to the road, shielding the private car park, tennis court, and communal garden. In 1989 the building won the Architectural Brickwork Award. That same year it was criticised by the Prince of Wales, who called it 'aggressive-looking'. Nevertheless, English Heritage listed it Grade II in 2018 for, among other reasons, its reinvention of high-rise living.

6

Source: Tjerk Ruimschotel (all pictures)

**Grand Union
Canal Walk Housing**
Grand Union Walk and
Kentish Town Road, Camden
Grimshaw
1988
🔴 Camden Town

In Grand Union Walk Housing, Nicholas Grimshaw's practice demonstrated that the High-Tech architectural repertoire could also be employed for terraced housing. The single-aspect, north-facing row of houses were the result of a need to use a leftover strip of land in a larger project for a Sainsbury's supermarket. Although just ten metres wide, the strip running parallel to the Grand Union Canal accommodates ten three-bedroom houses. As part of the planning application for the supermarket, the municipal planners asked for a mixed-use scheme. Instead of the planned block of flats, the architects requested that the project consist of individual houses. Their wish was granted (Nicholas Grimshaw has since said that the client allowed them freedom with the design of the homes, never questioning

the saleability of the homes). At one end of the terrace there is a volume containing a one-bedroom maisonette and a studio flat, both with triangular floor plans. The houses have a closed wall to the south to stop vehicle noise from the supermarket car park. To allow in light, they all have a double-height living area with a glazed industrial door. This faces the canal and can be raised to create an outdoor space with the balcony, which juts out over the water. In addition, light enters the first floors from skylights. In 2006, a roof terrace was added to each of the ten homes.

A private footpath along the canal gives access to the front doors of this miniature gated community. The houses and the supermarket were listed Grade II in 2019.

6

Comyn Ching Triangle

Area between Shelton Street,
Mercer Street, and Monmouth
Street, Camden
Terry Farrell & Partners
1978–1991
⊖ Covent Garden

081 B

In the 1970s, when 'tabula rasa' planning was the dominant ideology and Covent Garden was on the brink of full-scale demolition in the name of urban renewal, community action, listing, and forward-thinking postmodern interventions helped save the neighbourhood. The emerging ideas of conservation and regeneration are evident in Terry Farrell's design for the Comyn Ching Triangle. For more than a decade, he and his practice were involved in the multi-phase revival of a triangular block bounded by Monmouth Street to the west, Mercer Street to the north-east, and Shelton Street to the south-east. This block had previously been home to Comyn Ching ironmongers since the early eighteenth century, and had included various functions. Farrell's plan focused on retaining and integrating historic buildings: eighteenth-century houses were to be restored, new postmodern-style buildings were to replace the nineteenth-century

Corner of 45–51 Monmouth Street and 29–31 Mercer Street (listed)

Source: Philipp Meuser (all pictures)

buildings at the three corners, and the block's core was to be cleared of the disorderly mass of building extensions, to create a new urban space. Although the core (Ching Court) was planned as public square, reached by a public thoroughfare, it is now gated. Still, most of Farrell's exuberant works are visible today (though critics have observed their brilliance is in the fact that they are not too noticeable). The vulnerability of the architecture became apparent in 2016 when a plan was approved to change the building in Monmouth Street. The work converted the existing offices for residential use, so on the upper floors, the characteristic three-storey column of triangular bay windows was replaced with balconies. In protest, Farrell launched a campaign to save his work. The 2010s refurbishment highlighted the need to see the buildings as part of a complete project and to protect the integrity of the 1980s revival plan. The altered corner building unfortunately could not be listed, but Terry Farrell's other two corner blocks were listed Grade II in 2016. At the same time, two of the other buildings by Farrell within the area, 15–19 Shelton Street and 65–71 Monmouth Street, had their listings updated to reflect their place in the overall scheme.

6

Corner of 19 Mercer Street and 21 Shelton Street (listed)

Comyn Ching Triangle: The unlisted corner block (Monmouth Street and Shelton Street) after its conversion from offices to dwellings. The projecting three-storey column of bay windows and inset door were replaced by a plainer door and windows and small balconies on every floor.

6

Horselydown Square

Tower Bridge Piazza and
Brewery Square, Southwark
Julyan Wickham
1991
Ⓣ London Bridge

082 C

Horselydown Square is a high-density
mixed-use urban area designed around
two new pedestrian squares. It is situated on a site previously occupied by
the Anchor Brewery, near the southern
end of Tower Bridge. It is made up mostly

of housing (170 apartments in mainly five-storey blocks) but also includes retail and office space and underground parking. The postmodern buildings were designed by Julyan Wickham, who is currently a partner in Wickham van Eyck, which he runs with his wife Tess van Eyck. Van Eyck is the daughter of acclaimed Dutch architects Aldo and Hennie van Eyck, and the continental influence can be seen in the combination of various functions and vibrant forms in Horselydown Square. Wickham's new urban layout incorporates some existing buildings as well as entrances based on the original pedestrian routes leading to the River Thames. The curved yellow-brick walls and blue-painted balconies and window frames are nicely juxtaposed with the browns of the neighbouring warehouses of Shadwell. The round glazed corners and towers generate a certain nautical atmosphere. In 2015 a developer bought the scheme and refurbished parts of the offices and the shop fronts on the ground floor, improved the entrances to the flats, and repainted the window frames and walls. Instead of the initially planned three-storey office block on Tower Bridge Piazza (now Courage Yard), a one-storey pavilion was erected for a restaurant. The complex, which was bought by the Borough of Southwark in 2019, is not currently listed.

6

Source: Tjerk Ruimschotel (all pictures)

Shepherdess Walk
10–22 Shepherdess Walk,
Hackney
Henley Halebrown
1999
⊖ Old Street

083 C

This project, which received a RIBA Award in 2000, can be seen as one of the first architecturally satisfactory conversions of a warehouse into residential units in London. It was the result of a winning combination of an entrepreneurial client and a capable architect. The London-based practice Henley Halebrown had been established a few years earlier in 1995 after a series of informal collaborations. In 1997, the Manhattan Loft Corporation commissioned them to convert the building on Shepherdess Walk. The developer was run by Harry Handelsman, a businessman who had previously lived in New York. Inspired by the artists' way of life he had observed in Manhattan, he wanted to adapt the concept of loft living for London. He selected a site in Hackney, then a borough with many run-down structures and low prices. Named by the developer as The Factory, after Andy Warhol's famous New York studio, this conversion of a derelict industrial building quickly became a symbol

for a stylish lifestyle. It showcased the changing lifestyles that were to transform parts of London into 'creative districts' at the end of the millennium. Today the average asking price for properties on Shepherdess Walk is close to one million pounds sterling. The warehouse itself dates from the early twentieth century. It encloses a landscaped communal courtyard and rises to varying heights, five storeys in some places, four in others. There is commercial space on the ground floor and a basement-level car park. The 50 dwellings on the upper floors are reached by an elevator and via short galleries in the courtyard. Each of the 13 penthouses extends through former skylights up into a rooftop pavilion with a garden. The main material is brick, laid in stripes of brown and yellow. Iroko timber and zinc are used for the rooftop part of the building as they weather well. This rooftop area offers a somewhat suburban setting high above the city, allowing for chats over the fences between the penthouse gardens. Most of the flats – branded as lofts because of features such as exposed brickwork, huge windows, and high ceilings – were sold as raw industrial spaces to facilitate a design-conscious clientele in creating their own bespoke apartment.

6

Source: Bob Bronshoff (Gil Pictures)

Segal Close and Walters Way   084 E
1–7 Segal Close (off Brockley
Park), 1–13 Walters Way (off
Honor Oak Park), Lewisham
Walter Segal et al.
1982, 1987
🚉 Honor Oak Park

Often mistaken for prefabs or temporary dwellings, these houses offered a revolutionary approach to alleviating the long waiting lists generated by the housing crisis of the 1970s: people could build their homes themselves as part of a council-funded scheme. The straightforward timber-frame construction system was devised by the German-British architect Walter Segal (1907–1985). Before settling London in the mid-1930s, he had studied architecture in Berlin and lived in various places, including a utopian community in Switzerland, Cairo, and Mallorca. In the early 1960s, he married his second wife, Moran Scott, who owned a large Victorian house. Segal wanted to replace this with a modern, self-designed one. While demolishing the old home and constructing the new one, the Segal family lived in a timber structure they had built themselves on-site. It took just two weeks to erect and cost very little

(800 pounds sterling). This 'Little House in the Garden' generated more interest than the new brick house, leading to several private commissions that allowed Segal to refine the construction method. His approach centred on the use of standard-sized, easily accessible building components. Employing wood for the most part, the 'Segal method' avoided the need for brick-laying and plastering. The lightweight frames minimised the need for excessive foundations and specialist skills, and the houses could be configured to suit a family's individual needs. In line with his belief that 'anyone who could saw in a straight line could build a house', Segal designed an uncomplicated post-and-beam system that could be easily assembled by individuals with no previous construction experience. The roofs were covered with woodwool slabs and felt. The walls were also lined with woodwool and covered by compressed cement. The homes were on stilts to compensate for uneven terrain, a feature that also made maintenance and alterations easy. Although initially intended to be single-storey, the system could also be used to construct two-storey homes. A total of 200 of these houses were built in the 1980s, many of them in Lewisham

because of the council's self-build scheme – the first of its kind in the UK. The most exemplary among these were the homes on Walters Way and Segal Close, whose names were chosen by residents in tribute to the architect, who sadly died before Walters Way was finished. Segal Close, built between 1979 and 1981, is an enclave of seven single-storey houses. Approximately 20 minutes' walk away is Walters Way, a close of 13 two-storey houses erected between 1985 and 1987. In the 1970s Lewisham's Deputy Borough Architect Brian Richardson was instrumental in persuading the council to agree to support a housing scheme and to provide building sites. Sites unsuitable for conventional house building, because of their hilly terrain and mature trees, were made available to people on the housing waiting list, with the government lending the money for materials. In 1976, 168 people attended the meeting where it would be decided who could start with a self-built house. Fourteen participating families were selected by ballot, seven for the largest site (which became Segal Close) and seven for three other sites. The actual building work on Segal Close only started in 1979. Men, women, and children all helped with the building work.

Specialist contractors were hired to assist with laying drains, erecting structural frames, and moving and stacking building materials. Walter Segal, already in his seventies, planned the houses and provided the builders with simple freehand drawings. Although all houses have the same basic construction, they differ to suit the needs and wishes of the individual self-builders. However, being a modernist, Segal insisted on flat roofs. Many dwellings have since been adapted and extended and because of this changeable character, it is difficult to see how the buildings could be listed, as they probably should be. Despite the fact that they were erected later, the homes on Segal Close are also made from timber and woodwool slabs. The site is also on a slope: the road gently curves down a hill. The houses have private gardens and wooden decks. The shared roadway is both a car park and a social area, enjoyed by children and adults alike. Walters Way is known for its annual street party and collective Christmas festivities, as well as other celebrations, to which Segal Close residents are also invited. Many of the occupants of the 'Segal houses' open their doors to the public at London's annual Open House event, usually held every September.

6

Palm Housing Co-op
and Oxo Tower Wharf
Broadwall and Barge House
Street, Lambeth
Lifschutz Davidson
1994–1996
🚉 Waterloo East ⊖ Southwark

In the late 1970s, when the Pompidou Centre had been completed, and the construction of the Lloyd's Building was underway, Richard Rogers designed another development: a voluminous mixed-use complex consisting of a series of Lloyd's-like towers and a glazed pedestrian arcade on the south bank of the Thames. The prominent site was close to the National Theatre and Waterloo and Blackfriars bridges. After meeting with fierce opposition, Rogers' proposal for the 'megastructure' was abandoned (and later became one of the great unbuilt schemes for twentieth-century London). During the so-called Battle of Coin Street, an action group successfully petitioned to secure a site of

5 hectares for social housing, community enterprises, and public green space rather than offices and commercial developments. The group, which later became Coin Street Community Builders (CSCB), managed to purchase the land from the Greater London Council (then facing collapse) for a token price in 1984. Since then, several projects have been completed on the original site and other locations nearby. The CSCB's first project was a traditionally designed low-cost building for the Mulberry Housing Co-operative, located between Coin Street and Bernie Spain Gardens. Constructed around a courtyard, it comprised 56 dwellings ranging from one-bedroom flats to four-bedroom houses. The CSCB wanted all the residential accommodation built on the Coin Street sites to be social housing, available at affordable rents to individuals and families in need. Priority is given to specific groups such as those working in low-paid jobs in central London. There are four different buildings on the site, each named after a housing

co-op: Mulberry (1988), Palm (1994), Redwood (1995), and Iroko (2001). Together, these organisations manage some 220 high-quality, affordable new homes. The tenants cannot purchase the properties, enabling the housing to remain available at reasonable rents. Half of the vacancies that arise at Palm, Redwood, and Iroko can be let to people who apply to the co-operatives directly. The other half must be offered to households put forward by Lambeth and Southwark councils. Mulberry is filled only via these local councils. After Mulberry, the CSCD ran architectural competitions for the next two projects in order to encourage high-quality architecture. Lifschutz Davidson were selected to build the first one, the Palm Housing Co-op. The firm, founded by Alex Lifschutz and Ian Davidson in 1986, completed the building along Broadwall in 1994. It consists of 11 three-storey family houses, as well as two four-storey bookend blocks and a nine-storey tower, which contain five two-bedroom flats, and ten one-bedroom

flats. The family houses were designed for flexible accommodation: they have sub-divisible living spaces at ground- and first-floor levels, and loft space for yet further expansion. Their pitched roofs allowed for loft storage space on the street side and a double-height top storey on the park side, while also lending the homes an individual look. The last two co-ops were built later: Redwood was part of the Oxo Tower Wharf refurbishment and Iroko was designed by Haworth Tompkins (086). The Oxo Tower project turned out to be the CSCB's most ambitious project and the funds generated by it allowed the organisation to invest money back into the area. Originally built around 1900 as a power station, the tower was adapted by the company that manufactured the Oxo stock cubes in the 1920s. Its architect, Albert Moore, extended the riverside façade and designed the logo into the windows to skirt some of the advertising prohibitions of the time. When the CSBC purchased the building in the 1990s, it was for the most part derelict and part of the site was a helicopter pad. The ambitious project was for a mixed-use development: the Redwood Housing Co-op plus some commercial premises, both of which were accommodated while maintaining the building's original shell. On the ground floor, there are shops, art galleries, and within the building contours, one of the first public arcaded walkways along the Thames. On the first and second floors are designer workshops. Five floors of the wharf accommodate 78 flats, which range from one- to three-bedroom homes. A spectacular new glass rooftop extension, contrasting with the brick volume of the main building, houses a 400-seat restaurant. Although the wharf is widely regarded as an iconic symbol on the South Bank, it is not currently listed.

6

Iroko Housing Co-op
Upper Ground, Cornwall Road,
and Coin Street, Lambeth
Haworth Tompkins
2001
🚌⊖ Waterloo

086 C

This project was constructed parallel to the redevelopment of the Oxo Tower Wharf and by the same organisation, Coin Street Community Builders (CSCB; 085). The client wanted to utilise the site's potential for large family homes and also allow for smaller households in order to generate a mixture of occupants. Outdoor space was vital: every dwelling had to have its own space and there had to be a shared garden for socialising. The organisation intended to retain the site's 260-space commercial underground car park, which offers a cross-subsidy for the affordable housing. They invited four young practices to prepare designs, and selected Haworth Tompkins, a firm founded by Graham Haworth and Steve Tompkins in 1991. To address the challenges and opportunities of the site, the architects created three blocks around a communal courtyard garden. The blocks contain 59 homes in total: 32 five-bed houses, 6 three-bed maisonettes, 21 one- and two-bed maisonettes and flats. All dwellings have their own outside space, ranging from private gardens to balconies. The terraced houses on Coin Street and Cornwall Road are five-bedroom townhouses four

storeys high. The top storeys are set back to make room for the individual roof terraces overlooking the courtyard. On Coin Street, there are also two three-bedroom maisonettes with roof terraces and below them, at ground-floor level, a two-bedroom flat for wheelchair users. Along Upper Ground, three-storey houses with street-level front doors are topped by two-storey maisonettes, which are reached via a third-floor gallery on the inside of the block. The corners of the Upper Ground building are occupied by two shops at ground level. Above them are one- to three-bed flats and maisonettes. Iroko Housing Co-op was completed in 2001 and officially opened by the Mayor of London in 2002. The fourth

side enclosing the courtyard garden was added later: Coin Street Neighbourhood Centre in Stamford Street, also by Haworth Tompkins, the first construction phase of which was finished in 2007. The building houses various separate but interlinking functions, including a nursery with an outdoor playground, a space for youth clubs and after-school activities, two floors for community (e.g., for education or meetings) and business use, a community café, a commercial restaurant, a roof terrace, and offices for the CSCB. A cast-concrete staircase connects the functions internally. The second construction phase will occupy the land at the junction of Cromwell Street and Stamford Street.

6

Contemporary

From 2001 to the Present

BedZED
Helios Road, Sutton
ZEDfactory/Bill Dunster
2002
🚊 Hackbridge

087 A

Although BedZED is almost two decades old, it remains one of the few residential developments in London (or even the UK) where environmental measures are visually prominent features of the building. More recent projects often achieve high sustainability scores based on the nature and thickness of the construction and the use of energy-saving installations, without this aspect being significantly reflected in their architectural expression. The Beddington Zero (Fossil) Energy Development (BedZED for short) incorporates other uses: there are 2,500 square metres of commercial space, situated for the most part on the north side of the blocks, besides the 82 dwellings. In terms of housing, it includes both large and small apartments and maisonettes, nearly all with a garden, balcony, or roof terrace. The high-density suburban scheme was implemented for the largest housing association in London, Peabody. The project's main focus was, as its name implies, on minimising energy consumption. Energy was to come only from renewable sources on-site, such as solar panels, wood-pellet boilers, and a wood-fired combined heat and power plant. The buildings are oriented south to make full use of solar gain and are equipped with triple glazing and thermal insulation to keep heat in. Recycled or renewable building materials were all sourced from

within 80 kilometres of the site. Rain-
and wastewater are recycled. The project's smart architecture, with its high
level of finishing and abundant light,
was intended to attract urban professionals looking for a more eco-conscious
lifestyle. Innovative plots and access
patterns were tested, such as keeping
parking spaces on the edge of the neighbourhood. There was a strong emphasis
on jointly arranging car transport (pref-
erably electric). Although the scheme
has been successful in reducing electricity and mains-water usage, some of its
sustainability measures, such as the water treatment plant, have been uneco-
nomic, due to its limited scale. BedZED
is one of the many ZED projects undertaken by architect Bill Dunster and his office, ZEDfactory. The architects' design
was developed for Peabody in collaboration with the engineers Ellis & Moore and
Ove Arup, the sustainability consultants
BioRegional, and the construction consultants Gardiner & Theobald. The project was the first in which the local government sold land below market value
because of its sustainability ambitions.
Half of the homes were for rent from the
council or available for shared ownership
and the other half were sold on the open
market. BedZED was nominated for the
2003 RIBA Stirling Prize and has received
various awards for its green credentials.

7

Donnybrook Quarter
Eden Way, Tower Hamlets
Peter Barber
2006
🚇 Bow Road

088 C

With this rather small project of 40 units, completed in January 2006, Peter Barber emerged almost overnight as the housing architect of the new millennium. The Donnybrook Quarter won a RIBA Regional Design Award and was longlisted for the 2006 Stirling Prize, and Barber went on to receive *Building Design* magazine's Affordable Housing Architect of the Year the following year. This project resulted from a 2001 international architectural competition, entitled Innovations in Housing, run by the Architecture Foundation for the housing association Circle 33. The latter was established in 1968 by David Bernstein and David Levitt together with

their partners. The two men had worked together on the Brunswick Centre (063), founding their joint practice afterwards. Levitt Bernstein initially focused on projects for the housing association, aiming to design high-quality, affordable dwellings, mainly through conversions of run-down Victorian houses. By 2001, Circle 33 was one of the largest housing associations in the UK. The brief for Innovations in Housing was to develop new open-plan types for social housing. Peter Barber's design for a low-rise, high-density, street-based ensemble was chosen out of around 150 entries. The Donnybrook Quarter, located at the intersection of Old Ford Road and Parnell Road, consists of 40 dwellings. Three terraces form the core of the scheme. One faces Parnell Street while the other two stand either side of a new street, Eden Way. This pedestrian route expands at the northern end, creating a

square, spatial connections with adjacent neighbourhoods, and a short cut for local residents. The block perpendicular to the three terraces accommodates three oddly-shaped detached houses (two one-bedroom and one two-bedroom) and a tower-like four-storey apartment building on its triangular plan. The building blocks are angled and curved, and the ends of the terraces contain further unusually-shaped dwellings, some over workshops. In terms of housing construction, Barber's most innovative idea is the stacked hybrid terrace/courtyard housing type: the 'notched terraces', which at Donnybrook contain 28 dwellings. At ground-floor level a typical unit features one two-bedroom flat with a large open-plan living area and a fully glazed screen that gives access to a rear courtyard. Above the flat is a maisonette, entered from the street via a gated external staircase which leads up to the

roof terraces in the 'notches' between the units. The living area in the maisonettes has a glazed screen which faces south over the roof terrace. On the second floor there are two bedrooms, a bathroom, and a balcony facing the street. Barber planned the streets to be just 7.5 metres wide and lined by low-rise buildings to give them a human scale. He followed an 'eyes on the streets' philosophy: balconies and bay windows look onto the public realm to generate a safer, more social environment. Stairs, roof gardens, and the many front doors link the public space of the street with the private sphere of the residents. Barber's sculptural ensemble of white rendered houses seem to appeal as much to the public as to architecture enthusiasts. He later noted: 'We were thinking, Le Corbusier, Adolf Loos, J. J. P. Oud; the residents were thinking, "Spain! Holidays! Marbella!" I'm completely happy with that.'

7

Highbury Square
Avenell Road, Islington
Allies & Morrison
2009

089 C

 Arsenal

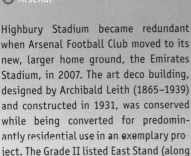

Highbury Stadium became redundant when Arsenal Football Club moved to its new, larger home ground, the Emirates Stadium, in 2007. The art deco building, designed by Archibald Leith (1865–1939) and constructed in 1931, was conserved while being converted for predominantly residential use in an exemplary project. The Grade II listed East Stand (along Avenell Road) and unlisted West Stand (behind the quaint two-storey terraces of Highbury Hills) were turned into apartment blocks. There is now a contemporary London (private) green square between them. The almost artificial looking turf for which Arsenal's groundspeople were famous is gone. In its place is a series of contrasting gardens (wild and manicured, high and low), designed in a grid pattern with a footpath alongside. New residential blocks replaced the North and South stands. These new-built flats are situated around courtyards connected to the central garden through large gates. This vast urban infill consists of 725 private homes and includes 25 different housing types. Highbury Square's architects, Allies & Morrison, founded by Bob Allies and Graham Morrison in 1984, have a reputation for thoughtful place-making. That is borne out in this project, which won a RIBA Regional Award in 2010.

7

One Hyde Park

090 B

100 Knightsbridge, Westminster
Rogers Stirk Harbour + Partners
2011

Knightsbridge

This high-end development caters for ultra-high-net-worth individuals (people with investable assets worth at least 30 million US dollars). Situated next to Knightsbridge Underground Station and connected to the neighbouring Mandarin Oriental Hotel, it incorporates apartments stretching the full width of the building and many other luxury facilities, as well as award-winning architecture – making it the most expensive address in London. One Hyde Park consists of four nine- to thirteen-storey interlinked 'pavilions', which are wider in the middle and narrower at the perimeter. This gives the development a lighter feeling and helps optimise views over Hyde Park. It was originally designed to house 86 apartments (including four penthouses), but during construction, several separate dwellings were purchased and merged into even bigger properties. Each apartment has two entrances: a main one for residents and their visitors, and another for staff and services (linked to the hotel via separate lifts). The development has private facilities for its occupants: a cinema, a swimming pool, squash courts, a golf simulator and gym, wine cellars, and a business suite with meeting rooms. There are three retail units at ground floor, which house firms such as McLaren Automotive

and Rolex. Apart from paying for 70 (much smaller) affordable homes some distance away, the development managers, Candy & Candy, provided the general public with a new pedestrian route through the site towards Hyde Park. They also moved the original underground station entrance next to the hotel. The project's architects, Rogers Stirk Harbour + Partners (RSHP), were originally called the Richard Rogers Partnership. The office was founded in 1977 and renamed in 2007 to reflect the contributions of Graham Stirk and Ivan Harbour. Stirk and Andrew Morris were the project partners for One Hyde Park. The project received a RIBA London Award in 2013. Other RSHP residential projects have also won RIBA awards, notably NEO Bankside (in 2012). When the former was shortlisted for the Stirling Prize in 2015, Architects for Social Housing protested, declaring the development subservient to abstract capital rather made for than local people.

7

Source: Philipp Meuser (all pictures)

Y:CUBE Mitcham

Clay Avenue and Woodstock Way,
Merton
Rogers Stirk Harbour + Partners
2015
Mitcham Eastfields

091 A

Developed for YMCA London South West, this affordable housing project by Rogers Stirk Harbour + Partners (RSHP) is as far away as one can get from One Hyde Park (090). The colourful complex of prefabricated dwellings, which cost 40 per cent less to build than the usual methods, provides short-term accommodation (normally three to five years) for young people unable to afford London's high rental costs. Y:Cube Mitcham consists of 37 prefab units: 36 self-contained one-bed flats plus one unit at one of the entrances as a communal space and office. The U-shaped scheme is composed

of three freestanding blocks: one five units wide and three units high situated on Woodstock Way, one three units wide and three high located on Clay Avenue, and one five units wide and part three, part two units high is placed perpendicular to Clay Avenue. Ground-floor flats on the streets have street-side front doors and those of the other block and the upper units are reached from the communal green courtyard. The access galleries are over 2 metres wide to encourage social interaction. Each unit has an area of 26 m² and contains a furnished living space with a small kitchen area and a separate bedroom with en-suite toilet and shower. They were manufactured off site using mainly renewable timber. RSHP created the modular system so units can be added or removed and transported for assembly at another site. The services (water, electricity, heating) are incorporated into each module and so can be easily connected to the facilities. Y:Cube Mitcham was the first Y:Cube development and has spawned related projects. While working on it, RSHP was asked by the Borough of Lewisham to come up with a plan for homeless families housed in inferior provisional accommodation. Local politicians and officials had been impressed by the Homeshell prototype at the 2013 exhibition 'Inside Out' at the Royal Academy. RSHP's design for the site of the former Ladywell Leisure Centre on Lewisham High Street was a temporary building of 24 two-bedrooms flats in 64 units, stacked four storeys high with community and retail units at street level. Completed in 2016, PLACE/Ladywell is 'a permanent housing solution in a temporary location': it can be moved a permanent site or divided up to cater for smaller projects. In 2019, a permanent scheme for the site was developed and it is now unclear what will happen to the prefab units. However, three new 'pop-up villages' are being planned in the borough. For Edward Street in Deptford, there is a design for 34 two- and three-bedroom in up to seven storeys. At Burnt Ash Hill in Lee, a part five-, part six-storey building is envisaged with 40 two- and three-bedroom flats. In Winchfield Road in Sydenham, four blocks are being planned. Although the developments in Lewisham are progressing, a second 31-unit YMCA Y:Cube, coupled with a new community centre in Chessington, Kingston, is currently experiencing planning problems.

7

Y:CUBE Mitcham: Temporary prefab dwellings designed by
Rogers Stirk Harbour + Partners for YMCA London South West
in a suburban corner of Merton

Peabody Avenue
Turpentine Lane, Westminster
Haworth Tompkins
2011
⊖ Pimlico

When it was constructed in the late 1870s, Peabody Avenue was one of the most radical projects implemented by Henry Darbishire (1825–1899) for what was then the Peabody Trust (now the Peabody housing association). Darbishire adapted his design for a standard tenement block for the strip of land: the development consisted of 26 staircase-access blocks aligned in two straight rows stretching around 300 metres along a railway line. All blocks were freestanding but abutting, and thus only had windows on the long façades. The heights ranged between four and five storeys.

The three freestanding buildings to the south of the avenue, in Peabody Close, were erected in the 1880s. In the 1940s, Second World War bombing damaged the southern end of the avenue, destroying four blocks there and one in Peabody Close. Over the years, the estate was developed in a piecemeal fashion. In the 1990s, two blocks were partially repaired and inhabited but then demolished in 2009. Several proposals for the redevelopment of the area failed until the current scheme was adopted and planning permission was granted in 2008. After lengthy negotiations with residents, planners, and English Heritage, Peabody and architects Haworth Tompkins were given the go-ahead to erect 55 homes on the bomb-damaged part of the site. The new L-shaped intervention extends one of the existing rows and encloses

Source: Tjerk Ruimschotel (all pictures)

7

the southern end of the avenue. It consists of two six-storey buildings. A double-height gateway in the short side of
the 'L' makes for a grand entrance. The
new brick façades extend up to five storeys, matching the existing walls in terms
of height. The original roofs are continued in the dark-coloured recessed top
storey. Sleek, simple windows puncture
the solid wall of stock bricks in various
warm colours. This level accommodates
eight wheelchair-accessible apartments.
The short side of the 'L' comprises a community centre on the ground floor and
four one-bedroom flats on each of the upper storeys. This block has a central staircase and lift. The longer block consists of
a main volume and two end volumes, all
slightly curved so the ensemble traces
the form of the railway line for a less severe feel. There is a large proportion of
three-bed apartments in the development. These have cantilevered balconies.
As part of the scheme, the outdoor spaces
were also rejuvenated. Landscape architects Coe Design preserved the plane
trees that run down the avenue and designed a play park and a community garden. The outdoor spaces such as the children's play park are recessed, providing
privacy. In the exterior appearance of the
building, the various housing types and
community centre are barely visible.

Darbishire Place
John Fisher Street,
Tower Hamlets
Niall McLaughlin
2014
🚇 Tower Hill

Opened in 1881, this Peabody estate originally consisted of 11 blocks, providing 286 flats for 1,200 people. It was built as part of a series of ten estates erected by the housing association to replace slums. Its name reflects its original architect, Henry Darbishire. Four of the blocks were arranged in a square, surrounding a courtyard. One of these was destroyed during the Second World War. Niall McLaughlin's new building stands on the site of this block. The building conforms to the elevations and volumes of the existing buildings but is somewhat longer. One end is tapered and retains the historic permeability of the estate by leaving the corners open. Wide loggia balconies enliven the geometry of the walls. Entrance to the flats is from the courtyard, and a naturally lit winding staircase provides access to the 13 dwellings, which are of five different types. The ground floor comprises one two-bedroom and one three-bedroom apartment. The first floor accommodates one three-bedroom and one four-bedroom apartment. The second, third, and fourth floors each have a single one-bedroom apartment over the entrance at the courtyard side, and two triple-aspect two-bedroom apartments at the ends. The architect initially chose a grey brick to match the soot-stained London brick. But when Peabody decided to clean the exteriors, McLaughlin changed his order to a matching pale colour, one which still contrasts with the white concrete bands around the windows and loggias.

One Church Square

2–6 Moreton Street,
Westminster

PDP

2013

🚇 Pimlico

094 D

One Church Square is a part four-, part five-storey building comprising 39 apartments. The building is planned around a central courtyard covered by a glass canopy. The fourth floor includes a landscaped roof garden for all of the building's occupants in order to enhance social interaction and to promote a sense of community. The client, the charitable foundation Dolphin Living, commissioned the architects to provide housing for key workers as well as some apartments for rent on the open market. For key workers, there are 4 studios and 14 one-bedroom, 11 two-bedroom, and 2 three-bedroom apartments. The other units comprise 3 one-bed and 5 two-bed apartments. The entrance is located off the public square that the estate shares with a Grade I listed church, St James the Less. This strengthens the connection between the two buildings. The link is also reinforced by the similar palette of materials. One Church Square is situated next to the conservation area of the Lillington Gardens Estate (064), and the choice to use red brick also respects these surroundings. To reach Level 4 of the Code for Sustainable Homes, the architects integrated a variety of features. The building has rooftop solar panels to produce electricity as well as an airtight envelope and mechanical ventilation with a heat recovery system. The horizontal and vertical brise-soleils in aluminium are energy-saving but also contextual: the pattern of perforations is taken from an image of St James the Less. All units are designed to be of the same high standard: the only difference between the affordable and market-rate flats is the inclusion of a dishwasher in the latter.

7

Source: Philipp Meuser

One Church Square: The landscaped communal
roof garden covered by a glass canopy

7

Copper Lane

1–6 Copper Lane, Islington
*Henley Halebrown Rorrinson
(HHbR)*
2014

🚇 Arsenal

Completed in 2014, Copper Lane is the first modern, architecturally interesting example of co-housing in London. Such housing projects have self-contained private dwellings but also community space. They are run by their residents and usually also built by them. Copper Lane is a development of six houses, with areas ranging from 70 to 155 square metres. The ensemble, in the inner area of a block of terraces, is set back from the site boundaries. The houses are arranged around a central upper-ground-floor courtyard, situated over a single-storey communal space, which houses a shared laundry, workshop, and a hall with an area of 50 square metres. A continuous communal garden surrounds the houses on the exterior perimeter. The two two-storey

houses have brick façades, and the four three-storey houses are clad in untreated wood. The individual houses are owned on 999-year leases, by leaseholders who are also directors of the firm that owns the site and communal space as a freehold. Two of the current occupants were originally residents nearby. They began the project in 2008, when they noticed that the site was up for sale. With only a short time to make an offer, they established a company and bought the abandoned set of buildings. At that time, there

was no planning permission, only a hint from the planning officers that they might consider residential occupancy. A small car-free path leads from Springdale Road to the site. The development is behind a gate, but it is not a gated community. The clients did not adopt any particular philosophy, beyond the basic principle of co-housing, which for them was about people organising to build and live together. Since the site and lifestyle did not seem fit for any of the traditional London housing typologies, the group and the

7

Source: Bob Birdsnow

architects took the opportunity to explore different architectural solutions. After ten architectural practises were interviewed, they chose Henley Halebrown Rorrinson in 2009. Their idea was that a co-housing scheme should be more than conventional homes with the addition of communal facilities and that they should find a new typology. Before settling on the arrangement of hardly distinguishable individual houses, the architects had proposed a single large villa, carved up internally into homes. When construction started in 2013, all building materials including the long spans of the timber frame, window frames weighing over

Copper Lane: The central upper-ground-floor courtyard situated over the co-housing project's communal facilities

half a tonne, and 50 tonnes of topsoil had to be transported down a 50-metre-long, 2.5-metre-wide lane. Parts of the houses are sunk into the ground to ensure that the building height stays below the predominant height of the elevation of the neighbouring houses. To achieve energy efficiency, the design includes a well-insulated structure, triple glazing, and solar thermal water heating, among other sustainable features. On financial and environmental grounds, the clients agreed on a car-free development with the council, meaning that residents cannot park vehicles on-site or receive permits for on-street parking.

7

Source: Bob Bronshoff

Ely Court
Chichester Road and Gorefield
Place, Brent
Alison Brooks Architects
2015
 096 B

⊖ Kilburn Park

Following the proposals of the South
Kilburn Estate Regeneration Masterplan,
Canadian-born Alison Brooks replaced
two post-war three-storey freestanding
blocks of flats with new buildings containing 43 dwellings. The new houses of

Ely Court form a traditional street with
the existing houses along Chichester
Road, in an area which has been beset by
social problems since the late 1980s. The
new scheme consists of three parts, which
together help define a green space opening to the street on one side. The first,
to the west of this small public park, is
a four-storey 'flatiron' building of four
social-housing apartments adjacent to
a nineteenth-century pub. The second is
a block of 25 private-sector apartments
over maisonettes with gardens, following

the line of Chichester Road. To the rear of the second part, across a green space, is the third: a mews of 14 social-rent dwellings. Pedestrians are drawn into the estate by the open space. Thinning out the densely-packed post-war modernist buildings has helped bring people onto the estate. The homes themselves are a mixture of types: from one-bedroom apartments to houses with gardens. The ends of the buildings and the flatiron building in particular have an abundance of balconies and fenestration to ensure

good visibility over the park. Ely Court received a RIBA National Award in 2016 and was a finalist for the European Mies van der Rohe Award the following year.

Trafalgar Place

Rodney Road, Southwark
de Rijke, Marsh, Morgan Architects
2015

⊖ Elephant & Castle

Trafalgar Place is designed to be the flagship housing project in the redevelopment of the Elephant and Castle area. It is the first phase and is supposed to alter the built environment while taking into account the history of the adjoining architecture. However, the redevelopment plan, commissioned by Southwark Council and managed by developers Lend Lease, completely wiped out the monumental Heygate Estate (Tim Tinker, 1974) over the period from 2011 and 2014. Many residents were issued with compulsory purchase orders and had to leave the estate, which had had a notorious reputation but had also provided social housing for thousands of residents. London-based architects dRMM, founded by Alex de Rijke, Philip Marsh, and Sadie Morgan, reflected on the bigger picture, consulted locals to see what residents wanted, and found out what would be the best fit in

the context through massing studies. This resulted in 235 tenure-blind dwellings in a mixture of mini-towers, apartment blocks, and town houses, of which a quarter count, on paper, as affordable housing. All homes have a garden, a balcony, or a roof terrace. Trafalgar Place also provides new public spaces: a woodland walk, thoroughfares, and a central square, which covers a subterranean car park. The estate's trees were also retained. The multi-coloured brickwork on the houses contributes to a more friendly atmosphere than had been present on the Heygate. dRMM also demonstrated their commitment to environmental awareness by constructing two buildings made from cross-laminated timber. RIBA London and National Awards in 2016 acknowledged the exemplary quality of the architecture. Architects for Social Housing, however, protested against the nomination of the project for the 2016 Stirling Prize. They criticised the role of architects in what they saw as social cleansing: according to the redevelopment plan, only 82 of the 2,532 new homes are to be council houses.

Source: Tjerk Ruimschotel

246

Walmer Yard
235–239 Walmer Road,
Kensington and Chelsea
Salter Collingridge
2016
⊖ Latimer Road

Walmer Yard was Peter Salter's first residential building in the UK. A student and later employee of Alison and Peter Smithson, he pursued similar ideas to the couple and attempts to follow them through in his built works. He taught at the Architectural Association and then several other institutions, perhaps gaining a reputation for being a 'paper architect' but in the process influencing generations of young architects. Salter was the principal designer for Walmer Yard, a project initiated by his former student the developer Crispin Kelly. Fenella Collingridge was design associate and Hugo Keene site architect. The scheme was 13 years in the making (of which seven years were taken up by construction), and its four houses ended up costing more than 5 million pounds sterling each. Although the original intention was to sell the houses – located on the edge of Notting Hill and thus of high value – Kelly set up a charity, the Baylight Foundation, to increase 'the public understanding of what architecture can do' through on-site events and workshops. The four interlocking houses are arranged around a courtyard and both rectilinear and curved stairwells. Two four-storey houses face the street on either side of the entrance. Behind them is a three-storey town house and to one side of it there is a two-storey house tucked behind the neighbouring semis. The lower ground floor has a garage for four cars, from which all four homes can be reached. Three houses have rooms on this floor: media rooms for the two dwellings at the front, and en suite bedrooms facing a private courtyard for the smaller house. Main entrances are on the raised ground floor. The two houses facing the street have kitchen/dining rooms at this level; the three-storey house has two bedrooms there, and the small house a kitchen-dining area and living room. Living rooms of the other three houses are on the second floor, in copper-clad tent-like constructions (likened to 'yurts' by the architect). The first floor is taken up by the bedrooms. The bulk of the building material is concrete, cast in-situ and moulded into complex shapes. A wide variety of materials for floors, walls, and details are added to this: timber screens and shutters; handrails made of leather twisted into ropes; wicker panels, tiling, and steel. The artistic qualities of the building might make it feel difficult to live in permanently, but enjoyable when inhabited temporarily. It is only fitting, therefore, that the Baylit Foundation now provides accommodation there for groups working in creative disciplines, including the visual and performing arts, the social sciences, architecture and urbanism, as an experiment in collective living. The houses are available to the general public for short stays.

7

Walmer Yard: Two of the street-facing fronts of the scheme
of four interlocking town houses made from cast concrete

Vantage Point
2 Junction Road, Islington
GRID
2016
🔴 Archway

099 B

Vantage Point is the new name for the refurbished Archway Tower, a 59-metre-tall 1960s office building which changed hands frequently over the years. Located above Archway Underground Station, the formerly dark building alongside empty shops and a chaotic traffic situation had created a poor urban environment. Rather than putting in a new request for planning permission, the client, the developer Essential Living, applied to transform the building into residential units for rent under Permitted Development Rights. The renovation of the tower as well as the provision of generous pedestrianised space has helped boost the regeneration of the area. The most noticeable improvement is the modification of the façade, which apart from imparting a striking aesthetic, improves thermal performance via the new cladding and helps eliminate downdrafts via protruding glass forms. The dark curtain wall has been replaced by a grid of two-storey-high aluminium frames, angled to reflect light and deflect wind, as well as to deter pigeons. Creamy stone cladding on what were previously black concrete end walls complements the light colour of the new façades. The former rooftop plant room became a two-storey bronze volume. It accommodates a games room and a gym on the top floor, with a view through the (partly) double-height dining room and communal lounge on the floor below. The total number of apartments is 118: 34 studios, 57 one-bedroom, and 27 two-bedroom units. The fifteenth floor is smaller and has six apartments. The floor plans for floors 2 to 14 are the same: two studio apartments, each with an area of 39 square metres; four one-bedroom apartments with an average size of 55 square metres; and two two-bedroom apartments, one of 70 square metres and another of 85 square metres. Both apartments are in the south-east corner and have windows cut in the solid end walls. The first floor is partly used for a meeting room and library with workstations. It also accommodates apartments. GRID architects, a practice established by Craig Casci in 2010, received a RIBA London Award for the project in 2017.

Source: Philipp Meuser (all pictures)

Dujardin Mews

Dujardin Mews, Enfield
Karakusevic Carson Architects,
Maccreanor Lavington Architects,
and East Architects
2017
🚊 Ponders End

100 A

A design team made up of Karakusevic Carson, Maccreanor Lavington, and East planned this redevelopment of part of a former gasworks in Ponders End. The homes in Dujardin Mews are the first new council-developed dwellings in the borough for 40 years and form part of Enfield's regeneration programme for the 1960s Alma Estate. The high quality of the

scheme has been widely recognised: the project, architects, and client have all received awards, including a RIBA National Award in 2017. Squeezed between the back gardens of nondescript suburban houses and the sports pitch and playground of a new-built school, Dujardin Mews is an almost traditional two-sided street of 38 social-rent and affordable houses. Because of the narrow width of the site, and to prevent houses overlooking the school grounds, the eastern terrace had to be composed of a new housing type. The western terrace protrudes slightly further than the eastern one and helps define the joint public space at the entrance to the adjoining school. At this protruding

end of the western terrace, there is a three-storey, flat-roofed block. One half of it contains four two-bedroom ground-floor courtyard apartments, on top of which are four two-bed maisonettes. In the other half of the block there are four four-bed three-storey town houses with their own gardens. The difference is hardly noticeable in the elevation. The remainder of the western terrace consists of 12 pitched-roof three-bedroom town houses with gardens. The eastern terrace mainly consists of eight three-bedroom detached houses without gardens. The kitchens are at ground level, with the living rooms on the first floor opening onto roof terraces which are situated on top of the garages between the houses. The notched form provides light and lends the street an unusual rhythm. The southern end of the western terrace is formed by a three-storey L-shaped apartment building containing six one-bedroom apartments. This building is called Valegro House after the Dutch warmblood gelding with whom the Enfield-born equestrian Charlotte Dujardin won multiple Olympic gold medals. As the client, the Borough of Enfield played a pivotal role in the success of the scheme. Whether it will serve as more than a pilot project for regeneration in the area remains to be seen. Hopefully, it will set an example for other councils to follow.

Source: Bob Bronshoff

Epilogue
Social Housing in London: Past, Present, and Future

Amy Visram

The coronavirus pandemic has shone a spotlight on London's decades-long housing crisis. Overcrowding seems to have contributed to high death rates: Brent and Newham – boroughs with extreme issues with overcrowding – had the highest mortality rates of all local authorities in England and Wales in the period from March to June 2020. In the year before that, average monthly rents hit record highs in Britain, reaching 1,425 pounds in London, with a median of 1,700 pounds in inner London and 1,295 in outer London.[1] Low and average earners can hardly afford to live in the city, where tenants spend an average of 40 per cent of their salary on rent. Yet the metropolis of almost 9 million people (and in Greater London 12–14 million) remains one of the most attractive cities in the world. As such, it has long been a target for international investors, who have been able to plough money into in the property sector practically uncontrolled since the 1980s.

Rogue landlords renting out sheds to multiple occupants, social-housing tenants being excluded from communal gardens, and galleries, coffee shops, and co-working spaces replacing chicken shops, churches, and factories – stories about the depressingly familiar situation abound. But what's to be done? With London's population projected to reach ten million by 2030, solutions are urgently required. Recent projects demonstrate that it is

possible to create high-quality social housing in Britain – the RIBA National Award-winning Dujardin Mews in Enfield or the Stirling Prize-winning Goldsmith Street in Norwich, to name just two. However, such projects represent a drop in the ocean. Given that London was renowned for its social housing across the globe during the first part of the twentieth century, a look back at its history might help us understand what went wrong – and bring potential solutions to the fore. The past projects outlined in this architectural guide

Redcross and Whitecross Cottages (Elijah Hoole, 1887–1890)

Totterdown Fields (LCC Architects' Department, 1901–1911)

Source: Bob Bronshoff

Boundary Street Estate (LCC Architects' Department, 1894–1900)

could perhaps offer us ideas for the future of both London and other growing metropolises worldwide.

Estates in London tend to be famous for their shortcomings rather than their architecture or innovations. And the terms 'council housing' and 'social housing' have a derogatory ring to them. 'Council housing' denotes public-sector homes let to those unable to pay private-sector rents or purchase a home. 'Social housing' refers to both council housing and homes run by housing associations – independent, not-for-profit organisations that build and run social housing projects – or other Registered Social Landlords. Although housing associations are private organisations, they are state regulated and receive government funding, a situation that has been in place since the early 1960s. In London they have been the main developers of new affordable homes since the 1980s, when they took over the task from the city's councils.[2]

Social housing in the UK has its origins in the philanthropist-built and run homes of the late nineteenth century. An early prototype for such a housing estate was Redcross Cottages and Whitecross Cottages built in Southwark from 1887 to 1890 (007). The Arts and Crafts-influenced cottages and community buildings were run by the social reformer Octavia Hill, one of the first social-housing managers. Hill's management system, whereby female voluntary workers collected rent weekly and got to know their tenants personally, meant that it was possible to intervene when, for instance, a house was overcrowded. Hill saw suitable housing and open spaces as vital for the health of Londoners, living in a packed city. Accordingly, the well-maintained houses were arranged around a village green, featuring a communal garden. Today, a city where one in seven social-housing households are overcrowded,[3] this model is perhaps particularly pertinent. Its architectural form and communal administrative concept made it possible to prevent overcrowding and provide open spaces.

At the turn of the twentieth century, local authorities became the main builders of social housing in Britain. The responsible body in the capital, the London County Council (LCC), built numerous housing projects during its existence from 1889 to 1965. Its first large-scale project was the Boundary Estate (011), which opened in 1900. Five-storey buildings replaced a six-hectare slum. The Arts and Crafts-style buildings are angled such that ample light and air can penetrate inside and the living rooms receive sunlight at least once over the day. There was a central laundry and workshops to foster local businesses. Yet the estate's success was limited: it rehoused around 1,100 fewer people than it displaced.[4] Since not many of the former slum-dwellers could afford the rents, the LCC subsequently started to build low-rise, low-density development in the suburbs: 'cottage estates' were built on or just outside the borders of the County of London. Examples include Totterdown Fields in Tooting (013), the first such estate, and Tower Gardens (014), the first cottage estate built 'out-county'.

The early cottage estates offered improved living conditions, green space, and high-quality design – although the rents also dictated that the residents have regular employment and be able to afford the commute into central London. Moreover, whether the successful elements of such low-rise, low-density schemes could be replicated or adapted for today's needs is debatable. The Future Spaces Foundation (a wing of Make Architects) estimated in 2015 that over the next 25 years London would require 67 new garden cities, each with a population of 30,000, to deal with the housing shortage. Such developments would represent a 17.6 per cent increase in the amount of land occupied by urban areas, and that's not including the necessary transport infrastructure. The foundation also notes that it 'takes 15–20 years to form a fully-fledged community', and eventually concludes that, though some

new garden cities or suburbs might be necessary, a more sustainable approach would be to increase the density of existing urban areas and improve people's quality of life in them.[5]

To cope with the acute housing shortage following the First World War, the LCC had to increase the density of housing in inner London, where space was limited. Ossulston Estate (031), for instance, was built on a narrow strip of land in Camden and made up of blocks ranging from three to six storeys in height. With its courtyard layout and clean modernist lines, the new design was likely influenced by the lead architect's visit to the Karl-Marx-Hof in Vienna. The estate had central heating, an electricity supply, and community facilities such as a coffee house and pub. Although it fell into disrepair over the years, it provided affordable housing for many at a time of urgency and moved away from the town planning norms of the time. It was renovated in 2004 – flats were enlarged to accommodate up-to-date standards – and is now listed.[6]

The continuing housing shortage after the Second World War meant that the LCC had to become more efficient. To achieve this, the Valuer's Department became responsible for housing, taking over from the Architects' Department. The new managers did not innovate; instead they continued to erect cottage estates, often

Source: Tjerk Ruimschotel

Ossulston Estate (LCC Architects' Department, 1929–1931)

with lacking transport links and facilities, and balcony-access blocks of flats, which were criticised by the architects of the time as being 'dull' and having an 'institutional appearance'. Open spaces and areas for the community tended to be omitted from the projects. In 1950, the Architects' Department once again took over the construction of housing, and in the ensuing period, the department became known as one of the most progressive and radical public architects' departments in the world.

The Loughborough Estate (050) was decisive in this return to innovation. Its high-rise blocks, constructed from reinforced concrete in a geometrical composition, are set in a landscaped setting straddling two streets. They thus form part of the urban environment. Some of the slab blocks take after Le Corbusier's Unité de Habitation. The construction methods – based on reinforced concrete and pre-fabricated panels – and geometric composition were decidedly modernist, but design decisions were made specifically to ensure good living conditions. However, over time, the estate did not quite go the way of the architects' utopian visions. Writing in 1972, Patrick Hodgkinson (the architect of the Brunswick Centre [063]) noted that the 'desolate space, conflicting scales, and social segregations produced soulless minimal homes.'[7]

From the mid-1950s, there was increased government funding on offer to housing schemes with blocks of over six storeys. Mixed-density estates – high- and low-rise buildings – seemed like the perfect solution to the lack of housing in the British capital. Low-rise estates were demolished and replaced with new ones according to the up-to-date town planning concepts. The success of these estates was as mixed as the densities.

One instance of a successful estate is the Golden Lane Estate (054), whose architects believed that a housing development should form part of the city and provide facilities for both residents and non-residents. Accordingly, the estate has generous, landscaped public areas and collective facilities. The blocks were arranged around courtyards, which helped foster social interaction and a

Source: Tjerk Ruimschotel

Loughborough Estate (LCC Architects' Department, 1953–1957)

feeling of community, as well as a feeling of safety. Despite the presence of a 16-storey tower block (Great Arthur House), the estate has not suffered from many of the social ills of other high-rise estates: levels of antisocial behaviour and graffiti are low. On construction, the estate housed a mixture of social classes. Today roughly 50 per cent of the homes are social housing and 50 per cent are privately owned. Perhaps the estate's central location, next to the Barbican (066) with its cinemas, theatre, gallery, and concert halls, and its well-off inhabitants working in the creative industries have helped it survive the test of time.

A decidedly less successful example is Thamesmead (062), a vast self-contained New Town erected on marshland on the eastern edge of London. Built by the LCC's successor, the GLC (Greater London Council), Thamesmead was planned as an area of mixed housing – from terraces to 12-storey tower blocks – for 60,000 people. As is well known, over time, Thamesmead became a notorious 'sink estate', with no central core, poor transport links, and a lack of amenities and social mix. Walkways, ground-level garages, and other parts of the estate became no-go areas. Empty homes attracted vandalism. The canals and lakes were not maintained. During the 1980s and 1990s standard brick houses were built around Thamesmead, fragmenting the area still further.[8]

Great Arthur House, Golden Lane Estate (Chamberlin, Powell & Bon, 1952–1962)

An attempt at regeneration is currently being led by the Peabody housing association in partnership with various local authorities. The plan is to build 20,000 homes, add new shops and culture and leisure facilities, create a new town centre, and maintain the waterways and parks – all on an area the size of the city of Winchester. Transport will also be improved: Crossrail and possibly the DLR will connect to the area in the coming years. How Peabody and its partners will see this through of course remains to be seen. In March 2020, the architecture critic Rowan Moore summed up the challenges for the project: 'The new new town will need, among other things, creativity. Thamesmead throws up singular situations: the margins of too-wide roads made into residential sites; the odd off-cuts of space left by concrete decks; the strange encounters of wilderness and infrastructure; the jumbling of private and public spaces – in which garden fences, for example, might back on to a putative town square – caused by its motley history. Generic solutions won't always work, and will miss the opportunities offered by the unique spirit of the place.'[9]

Thamesmead's brutalist aesthetics – arguably partially responsible for its decay – could become a selling point for young creatives unable to afford the rents in inner London. As the critic Owen Hatherley put it, 'This is basically a working-class Barbican, and if it were in EC1 rather than SE28, the price of a flat would be astronomical.'[10] Its open space might also be attractive after the recent lockdowns. Peabody's chief executive said in 2014 that Thamesmead 'has the potential to be London's major garden suburb, with beautiful green space, first-class amenities, excellent schools, and rapidly improving transport connections.'[11] If it's possible to retain some of the character of what's left of the original estate and to avoid pricing out residents, then Thamesmead could turn out to be an example of what a twenty-first-century garden suburb might look like.

The introduction of the Right to Buy in the 1980s had a big impact on the social-housing situation we see today in London. If a secure council tenant wanted to buy their home, they had the legal right to purchase it. Over time this depleted public housing stock, reducing in particular the number of large houses and high-quality properties. Council housing estates comprised both tenants and homeowners. Although not necessarily a negative point, this may have contributed to causing more of a divide in the 1990s: in better-off estates people bought their home, sold it and moved on, while those left behind in the less-well-off estates tended to be those on benefits or with

95 Peckham Road (Peter Barber, 2020)

social problems. The difficult economic conditions of the decade also meant that little was built. Since then, government policy has supported the transfer of the management of council housing to housing associations. Over the 2000s, demolition and renovation went hand in hand, house prices continued to rise, and luxury homes were erected on a large scale. It became almost impossible for many sections of the population to buy or rent a house in London.

So what sort of social housing is being built today and by whom? The short answer is not very much. According to the housing charity Shelter, 6,287 social housing units were built in the entire United Kingdom in 2018/2019.[12] That is almost fifteen times less than the number of units constructed in 1980, almost four decades before. There is a clear need for more social housing. And, as our look at history has revealed, the quality of these homes is just as important as the quantity if they are to last.

Various recent projects illustrate that it is possible for councils to build high-quality new homes. Enfield's first council housing in four decades, Dujardin Mews (100), a well-ordered street of red-brick houses in east London, is one such example. The scheme, a mixture of low-rise apartment blocks and houses, was constructed after consultation with residents and provides spacious interiors. It aims to encourage a sense of security and community through the positioning of homes, which face each other to foster interaction between residents. Like the Golden Lane Estate, the goal is to create a place, rather than just a set of houses.

Across London there are projects by architect Peter Barber: low-rise high-density Donnybrook Quarter (088) or 95 Peckham Road (2020) in Southwark, for example. The latter is a six-storey building, although it appears lower. At the rear are low-rise maisonettes. The bedrooms in the ground-floor maisonettes are located on the first floor to avoid disturbances from the busy street. There are generous roof terraces and a courtyard space for residents to meet and socialise. Brick is used here and in many of Barber's other projects, and it might be seen as a continuation of the norm. But a 2018 article describing Barber's McGrath Road project in Newham offers a good counter argument: 'At first glance, the tone of the bricks and mid-rise elevation imply a regular new London vernacular – the conservative style dominating new build housing across tenures and across the city. The detailing of Barber's project, however, feels more European. The double-height archways betray a hint of the Amsterdam School, while French doors beneath the chamfered lintel of a top-floor window

Donnybrook Quarter (Peter Barber, 2006)

provide generous natural light inside. What's more, there's not a pitched roof in sight. Instead, rectilinear forms dominate – in homage to one of Barber's heroes, Luis Barragán. The building looks like home, it looks like London. But it's somehow a different London, a London we've not yet arrived at.'[13] The mixture of familiar materials and unfamiliar elements and styles sets apart Barber's work. Squares, terraces, balconies, plazas, courtyards are frequently integral elements of his projects – a hopeful sign that the importance of outdoor space is returning to the forefront of affordable housing.

Alternative organisational models are also being explored today – and are indeed necessary to deal with the scale of London's housing crisis. Housing associations often work with private developers to build new estates or adapt existing ones. For the waterfront development in Thamesmead, for example, Peabody is working with the global real estate and investment group Lendlease. However, despite their potential, joint projects can result in the segregation of social-housing residents from those who own their homes or rent privately, through separate entrances or limited access to parks or gardens for social-housing residents. At Westbourne Place in Maida Vale, for instance, housing-association tenants were not permitted to use the gardens,

though after a media outcry the decision was reversed.[14] And if housing associations become reliant on private developers, the interests of their tenants might not be so well represented in the future.

Maintaining existing buildings or adapting old developments to remedy their deficiencies, as will potentially happen in Thamesmead, is another option for providing the necessary homes. But this needs to be done with respect for existing buildings and the communities occupying them. It would contribute to increasing the density in urban areas, a preferable alternative to establishing new garden cities, given the environmental concerns that go along with building on greenfield sites. Yet the solutions for densification need to be thoughtfully designed to provide suitable conditions for residents – and it's there that we can learn from the successes and failures of the past.

Dujardin Mews (Karakusevic Carson, Maccreanor Lavington, 2017)

Notes

1   Office for National Statistics, 'Private rental market summary statistics in England: April 2019 to March 2020', 17 June 2020, www.ons.gov.uk/peoplepopulationandcommunity/housing/bulletins/privaterentalmarketsummarystatisticsinengland/april-2019tomarch2020, acc. 15 Sept. 2020.

2   NLA Housing Insight Survey, 'New Ideas for London Housing', legacy.newlondonarchitecture.org/docs/nla_housing_essay.pdf, accessed 15 Sept. 2020. Here we should note the UK government's distinction between affordable and social housing: 'Affordable housing includes social rented, affordable rented and intermediate housing, provided to specified eligible households whose needs are not met by the market. It can be a new-build property or a private sector property that has been purchased for use as an affordable home.' See: www.gov.uk/government/collections/affordable-housing-supply, accessed 15 Sept. 2020.

3   Deborah Potts, 'How unravelling housing standards have contributed to the spread of COVID-19 in "rich" countries', 19 May 2020, www.kcl.ac.uk/how-unravelling-housing-standards-have-contributed-to-the-spread-of-covid-19-in-rich-countries, accessed 15 Sept. 2020.

4   Historic England, 'Arnold Circus, Bethnal Green', historicengland.org.uk/listing/the-list/list-entry/1001300, accessed 15 Sept. 2020.

5   Future Spaces Foundation, 'Vital Cities not Garden Cities: the answer to the nation's housing shortage?' 2015, www.futurespacesfoundation.org/wp-content/uploads/2016/04/Vital-Cities-not-Garden-Cities-FSF-dps.pdf, accessed 15 Sept. 2020.

6   Municipal Dreams, 'The Ossulston Estate, St Pancras: The English Karl-Marx-Hof?', 5 Feb. 2013, municipaldreams.wordpress.com/2013/02/05/the-ossulston-estate-st-pancras-the-english-karl-marx-hof, acc. 15 Sept. 2020; Simon Pepper, 'Pioneer Housing at Ossulston Street', Twentieth Century Society, Sept. 2007, c20society.org.uk/building-of-the-month/pioneer-housing-at-ossulston-street, accessed 15 Sept. 2020.

7   Cited in Mark Swenarton, Tom Avermaete, and Dirk van den Heuvel (eds), *Architecture and the Welfare State* (Abingdon and New York, 2015), p. 246.

8   Ariana Markowitz, 'The making, unmaking, and remaking of Thamesmead: A story of urban design, decline, and renewal in post-war London', DPU Working Paper, Nov. 2017, www.ucl.ac.uk/bartlett/development/sites/bartlett/files/the_making_unmaking_and_remaking_of_thamesmead._a_story_of_urban_design_decline_and_renewal_in_postwar_london.pdf, accessed 15 Sept. 2020.

9   Rowan Moore, 'The Reach, Thamesmead review – from sink estate to Thames des res', *Guardian*, 7 March 2020, www.theguardian.com/artanddesign/2020/mar/07/thamesmead-regeneration-london-the-reach-peabody-housing-association, accessed 15 Sept. 2020.

10 Owen Hatherley, *A Guide to the New Ruins of Great Britain* (London, 2010), p. 237.

11 BBC News, 'Thamesmead to get multi-million pound revamp', 29 March 2014, www.bbc.com/news/uk-england-london-26801368, acc. 15 Sept. 2020.

12 Shelter, 'The Story of Social Housing' n.d., england.shelter.org.uk/support_us/campaigns/story_of_social_housing, accessed 15 Sept. 2020.

13 George Kafka, 'Architect Peter Barber Is Reinventing London's Housing', *Metropolis*, 1 Nov. 2018, www.metropolismag.com/architecture/peter-barber-architect-profile, accessed 15 Sept. 2020.

14 Harriet Grant, 'Victory for residents of London estate after garden access row', *Guardian*, 12 Oct. 2019, www.theguardian.com/cities/2019/oct/12/victory-for-residents-of-london-estate-after-garden-access-row, accessed 15 Sept. 2020.

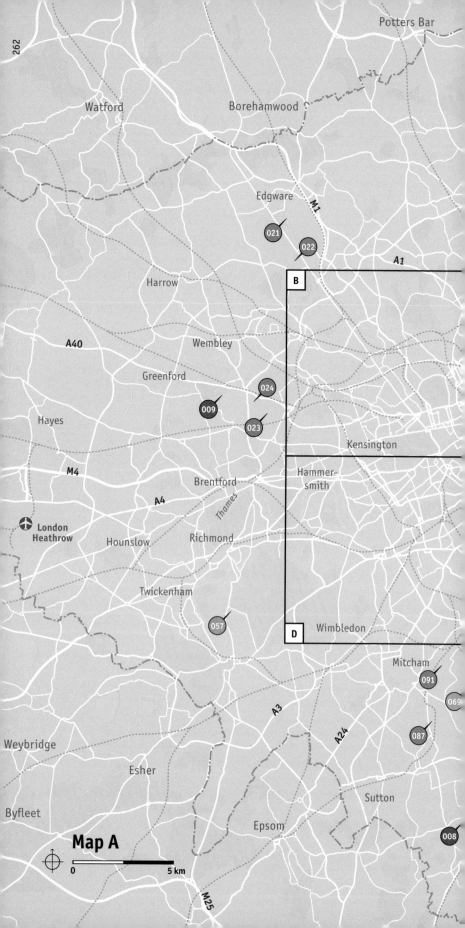

Potters Bar

Watford

Borehamwood

Edgware

M1

021

022

A1

B

Harrow

A40

Wembley

Greenford

024

009

023

Kensington

Hayes

Hammer-
smith

M4

Brentford

A4

Thames

London
Heathrow

Hounslow

Richmond

Twickenham

Wimbledon

D

Mitcham

091

057

069

Weybridge

A3

A24

087

Esher

Sutton

Byfleet

Epsom

008

Map A

0   5 km

M25

M25
Enfield
100
M11
Chigwell
014
026
A12
Romford
C
A10
Stratford
Ilford
020
025
Barking
A13
A11
City of London
Thames
062
Woolwich
028
A205
rixton
Greenwich
016
Lewisham
Bexleyheath
Dart-
ford
A20
Sydenham
E
Sidcup
Bromley
M20
A232
Orpington
M25
roydon
068

Map B

HARINGEY

Highgate

036

033

099 Archway

Upper
Holloway

074

030

Hampstead

029

Hampstead
Hampstead

005 071

Tuffnell
Park

ISLINGTON

Holloway Rd

Parkhurst Rd

Hampstead
Heath

037

Belsize Park

CAMDEN

Kentish
Town

Camden Rd

Finchley
Road &
rognal

Finchley
Road

Belsize Park

Kentish
Town West

Chalk Farm

044

Camden Road

Swiss
Cottage

Adelaide Rd

South
Hampstead

073

072

Abbey Rd

St. John's
Wood

Prince Albert Rd

027

Camden
Town

080

Mornington
Crescent

King's
Cross

St Pancras
Int.

031

King's Cross
St Pancras

Maida
le

Maida Vale

067

The Regent's Park

Albany St

Euston

Euston

063

Warwick
Avenue

Edgware Rd

Marylebone

Regent's
Park

Warren
Street

Euston
Square

Gower St

Russell
Square

Paddington

Paddington

Paddington

swater

Edgware Rd

Sussex Gardens

Marylebone

Edgware Road

Baker
Street

Baker St

Marylebone

Great
Portland
Street

Goodge
Street

001

Holborn

076

Wigmore St

Oxford St

Bond Street

Oxford
Circus

Tottenham
Court Road

081

Lancaster Gate

Marble
Arch

Covent
Garden

Bayswater Rd

eensway

Hyde Park

CITY OF
WESTMINSTER

Leicester
Square

Piccadilly
Circus

Charing
Cross

The Serpentine

090

056

Green
Park

The Mall

Thames

038

Hyde Park
Corner

Westminster

266

HARINGEY

Seven Sisters

South Tottenham

Hartingay

Harringay
Green Lanes

Stamford
Hill

Manor
House

Stamford Hill

Clapton Common

Finsbury
Park

Sisters Rd

Manor Rd

Stoke
Newington

Clapton

Lea Bridge R

Seven-

HACKNEY

Holloway
Road

Rectory
Road

089

Arsenal

095

Drayton
Park

Holloway Rd

Dalston
Kingsland

Hackney
Downs

Homer

Canonbury

Dalston
Junction

Hackney
Central

042

Highbury
& Islington

Caledonian Road
& Barnsbury

Essex Rd

Rd

London
Fields

ISLINGTON

003

Kingsland Rd

Haggerston

Upper St

New N Rd

Queensbridge

Cambridge
Heath

047

Angel

City Rd

083

Hoxton

055

058

046

011

Bethnal
Green

054

Old Street

Shoreditch
High Street

Bethnal
Green

Bloomsbury

Farringdon

066

Barbican

Commercial St

Whitechapel

Mile End Rd

Stepne
Gree

Chancery
Lane

Moorgate

Liverpool
Street

Whitechapel

TOWER HAMLETS

City
Thameslink

St. Paul's

CITY OF
LONDON

Aldgate

A13

Temple

Bank

Aldgate
East

Mansion
House

Fenchurch
Street

Shadwell

Blackfriars

085

Cannon
Street

Monument

Tower
Gateway

093

The Highway

086

London
Bridge

Tower
Hill

Map C

0   1 km

Waterloo
East

Southwark

Wapping

Waterloo

004

007

Borough

London
Bridge

London
Bridge

Tower
Bridge

082

Thames

Rotherhith

SOUTHWARK

St James Street
Whipps Cross Rd
Snaresbrook
WALTHAM FOREST
Lea Bridge Rd
Leyton Midland Road
Leytonstone
Lea Bridge
Leytonstone High Road
A12
Centre Rd
Hackney Marshes
Leyton
A12
Forest Ln
Stratford International
Maryland
Queen Elizabeth Olympic Park
Romford St
Hackney Wick
Stratford
Victoria Park
Stratford High Street
088
High St
A12
Roman Rd
Pudding Mill Lane
Abbey Road
Plaistow
Bow Church
West Ham
A11
Bow Road
Mile End
NEWHAM
Bromley-by-Bow
Burdett Rd
Devons Road
Star Lane
Barking Rd
TOWER HAMLETS
A13
Newham Way
Langdon Park
059
049
Canning Town
Poplar
Limehouse
Custom House for ExCel
061
Limehouse Link Tunnel
Westferry
All Saints
East India
West India Quay
Poplar
Blackwall
Royal Victoria
Canary Wharf
079
West Silvertown
Thames
Heron Quays
GREENWICH
Thames
South Quay
North Greenwich

St James's Park
032
012
094
064
Pimlico
077
092
045
Vauxhall
London Victoria
Gloucester Road
South Kensington
Sloane Square
King's Rd
KENSINGTON & CHELSEA
Thames
065
Battersea Park
Battersea Park
Battersea Bridge Rd
Imperial Wharf
Queenstown Road
Stockwell
Wandsworth Road
Thames
A3
Clapham High Street
Clapham North
Clapham Junction
St John's Hill
Battersea Rise
Clapham Common
Clapham Common
LAMBETH
WANDSWORTH
The Ave
Brixton Hill
Clapham South
King's Ave
Poynders Rd
A23
Trinity Rd
Wandsworth Common
035
Balham
arlsfield
034
Burntwood Ln
A214
A24
Streatham Hill
Tooting Bec
013
Garratt Ln
Tooting Broadway
Mitcham Rd
Streatham
Tooting
A23
Colliers Wood

TOWER HAMLETS

Crossharbour

Mudchute

Island
Gardens

Westferry Rd

Thames

Thames

Evelyn St

A102

Westcombe
Park

Trafalgar Rd

Cutty
Sark

Maze Hill

GREENWICH

Deptford

Greenwich

New Cross

New
Cross
Gate

Deptford
Bridge

Greenwich
Park

Shooters Hill Rd

St Johns

Elverson Road

A20

Lewisham

Blackheath

Brockley

Lee High Rd

Ladywell

Hither Green

Lee

Westhorne

Ave

LEWISHAM

084

Brownhill Rd

Catford

Stanstead Rd

Bromley Rd

Baring Rd

044

Bellingham Rd

018

Bellingham

048

Grove Park

019

Beckenham
Hill

A21

Lower
Sydenham

Beckenham
Place Park

New Beckenham

BROMLEY

Index of Architects

Digits indicate the project number

Index of Projects

Digits indicate the project number

Bibliography

Architectural Guides to London

Allinson, Ken, and Thornton, Victoria, *London's Contemporary Architecture* (London, 2014).

Burman, Sujata et al. *An Opinionated Guide to London Architecture* (London: Hoxton Mini Press, 2019).

Harwood, E., Saint, A., *London: Exploring England's Heritage* (London, 1991).

Hatherley, Owen (ed.), *The Alternative Guide to the London Boroughs* (London, 2020)

Jones, E., and Woodward, C., *Guide to the Architecture of London* (London, 2013).

Lambert, S., *New Architecture of London: A Selection of Buildings since 1930* (London, 1963).

McKean, C.,and Jestico, T., *Guide to Modern Buildings in London* (London, 1976)

Nairn, Ian, *Modern Buildings in London* (London, 1964).

Nairn, Ian, *Nairn's London* (London, 1966; repr. 2012).

Pevsner, Nikolaus, Cherry, Bridget, and Bradley, Simon, *The Buildings of England: London 1: The City of London* (4th edn, London, 1997).

_____ *The Buildings of England: London 2: South* (2nd edn, London, 1997).

_____ *The Buildings of England: London 3: North West* (2nd edn, London, 1991).

_____ *The Buildings of England: London 4: North* (2nd edn, London, 1998).

Pevsner, Nikolaus, Cherry, Bridget, and O'Brien, Charles, *The Buildings of England: London 5: East* (3rd edn, London, 2007).

Pevsner, Nikolaus, and Bradley, Simon, *The Buildings of England: London 6: Westminster* (3rd edn, London, 2003).

Whitehead, David, and Klattenhoff, Henning, *London: The Architecture Guide* (Salenstein, 2010).

Architecture and Housing in London

Allinson, Ken, *Architects and Architecture of London* (London, 2009).

Allan, John, *Berthold Lubetkin: Architecture and the Tradition of Progress* (London, 1992).

Beattie, Susan, *A Revolution in London Housing: LCC Housing Architects and Their Work 1893–1914* (London, 1980).

Billinghurst, Keith, *The Origins and Evolution of the Progress Estate: Eltham's Garden Suburb* (Bath, 2017).

Burke, David, *The Lawn Road Flats: Spies, Writers and Artists* (Woodbridge, 2014).

Chadwick, P., and Weaver, B., *The Town of Tomorrow: 50 Years of Thamesmead* (London, 2019).

Cherry, Bridget, and Robey, Ann, *Rediscovered Utopias: Saving London's Suburbs* (London, 2010).

Darling, Elizabeth, *Wells Coates* (London, 2012).

Daybelge, Leyla, and Englund, Magnus, *Isokon and the Bauhaus in Britain* (London, 2019).

Grahame, Alice, and Wilkhu, Taran, *Walters Way & Segal Close: The Architect Walter Segal and London's Self-build Communities – A Look at Two of London's Most Unusual Streets* (Zurich, 2017).

Guillery, Peter, and Kroll, David (eds), *Mobilising Housing Histories: Learning from London's Past for a Sustainable Future* (London, 2017).

Honer, Julian (ed.), *London Suburbs* (London, 1999).

Knox, P., *Metroburbia: The Anatomy of Greater London* (London: Merrell, 2017).

Lever, Judith, *Home Sweet Home: Housing Designed by the London County Council and Greater London Council Architects 1888–1975* (London, 1976).

Olechnowicz, Andrzej, *Working-class Housing in England between the Wars: The Becontree Estate* (Oxford, 1997).

Orazi, Stefi, *The Barbican Estate* (London, 2018).

Phipps, Simon, *Brutal London* (Tewkesbury, 2016).

Powers, A., *2 Willow Road, Hampstead* (rev. edn, London, 2004).

Simms, Barbara, *Eric Lyons & Span* (London, 2006).

Swenarton, Mark, *Cook's Camden: The Making of Modern Housing* (London, 2017).

Wagg, Christine, and McHugh, James, *Homes for London: The Peabody Story* (London, 2017).

Architecture and Housing in Britain

Boughton, John, *Municipal Dreams: The Rise and Fall of Council Housing* (London, 2018).

Burnett, John, *A Social History of Housing 1815–1985* (2nd edn, London, 1986).

Colquhoun, Ian, *RIBA Book of British Housing: 1900 to the Present Day* (2nd edn, Oxford, 2008).

Hanley, Lynsey, *Estates: An Intimate History* (London, 2007).

Harwood, Elain, and Davies, James O., *England: A Guide to Post-war Listed Buildings* (London, 2010).

Jensen, Finn, *Modernist Semis and Terraced Houses* (Burlington, VT, 2012).

Manley, Christine, *Frederick Gibberd* (London, 2017).

Orazi, Stefi, *Modernist Estates: The Buildings and the People who Live in them Today* (London, 2015).

Swenarton, M., *Homes Fit for Heroes: The Politics and Architecture of Early State Housing in Britain* (London, 1981).

Warburton, Nigel, *Ernö Goldfinger: The Life of an Architect* (London, 2004).

Online References

www.archdaily.com
www.architectsforsocialhousing.co.uk
www.architectsjournal.co.uk
www.acgthhoesibh.wordpress.com
www.c20society.org.uk
www.daveanderson.me.uk/houses/london.html
www.historicengland.org.uk
www.ideal-homes.org.uk
www.londongardensonline.org.uk
www.modernarchitecturelondon.com
www.modernism-in-metroland.co.uk
www.modernistestates.com
www.municipaldreams.wordpress.com
www.openhouselondon.org.uk
www.themodernhouse.com
www.towerblock.eca.ed.ac.uk
www.utopialondon.com
www.victorianweb.org/art/architecture/homes/index.html

Photos in this guide are by Bob Bronshoff, Philipp Meuser, and the author.
Seen here is the Dutch photographer Bob Bronshoff (born 1958) at work.

Source: Tjerk Ruimschotel